TRUE COLORS

An EFL Course for Real Communication

Basic

Jay Maurer
Irene E. Schoenberg

Joan Saslow
Series Director

LONGMAN

True Colors: An EFL Course for Real Communication   BASIC

Addison Wesley Longman, 10 Bank Street, White Plains, NY 10606

Editorial director: Allen Ascher
Director of design and production: Rhea Banker
Development editor: Jessica Miller
Managing editor: Linda Moser
Production manager: Marie McNamara
Senior Production editor: Lynn Contrucci
Production editor: Liza Pleva
Senior manufacturing supervisor: Patrice Fraccio
Cover design: Rhea Banker
Text design: Word & Image Design
Text composition: Word & Image Design
Illustrations: Pierre Berthiaume, Jocelyn Bouchard, France Brassard,
    Patrick Fitzgerald, Brian Hughes, Stephen MacEachern, John Mantha,
    Paul McCusker, Dave McKay, Dusan Petricic, Stephen Quinlan,
    Teco Rodrigues, Philip Scheuer, Margot Thompson
Photography: Gilbert Duclos

Library of Congress Cataloging-in-Publication Data

Maurer, Jay.
    True colors: an EFL course for real communication/Jay Maurer; Irene E.
    Schoenberg; Joan Saslow, series director
        p. cm.
    1. English language—Textbooks for foreign speakers.
2. Communication.   I. Schoenberg, Irene.   II. Saslow, Joan M.   III. Title.

PE1128.M3548   1998

428.2'4—dc21   97-12071
                                                                    CIP

ISBN: 0-201-18730-2

1 2 3 4 5 6 7 8 9 10—WC—03 02 01 00 99 98

Contents

Scope and Sequence of Specific Content and Skills (See also pages 140–145)

Listening	Expansion Activities	Personal Expression
Types: • spelling of names • conversations about names and occupations **Comprehension Skill:** • focus attention	• Game (reinforces *yes-no* questions and answers with *be*)	• talk about your own occupation
Types: • statements about phone numbers • a phone call to information **Comprehension Skill:** • focus attention	• Game (reinforces letters and numbers) • Game (reinforces statements with *be*)	• talk about your family and friends
Types: • addresses • a conversation in a classroom **Comprehension Skill:** • focus attention	• Game (reinforces adjective use) • Reading: business cards • Writing: business cards	• talk about where you live • give your classmate a compliment
Types: • a recorded announcement at a theater • a telephone message **Comprehension Skill:** • focus attention	• Game (reinforces asking and answering *wh-* and *yes-no* questions)	• invite a classmate to a real event
Types: • descriptions of activities • a telephone conversation **Comprehension Skills:** • focus attention • determine context	• Inter-Action (reinforces *wh-* questions in the present continuous) • Reading: a letter • Writing: a letter	• talk about what your family and friends are doing right now
Types: • sentences • a conversation about food **Comprehension Skills:** • recognize sounds • determine context • focus attention	• Reading: a menu • Writing: sentences about what a partner wants	• talk about foods you like and dislike
Types: • a description of what people are wearing • a conversation between two students **Comprehension Skill:** • focus attention	• Reading: a description of what someone is wearing • Writing: a description of a classmate's style	• talk about clothes and colors you like and dislike
Types: • conversations about ailments • a conversation with a doctor **Comprehension Skills:** • recognize sounds • focus attention	• Reading: a chart of health dos and don'ts • Game (reinforces health vocabulary and social language)	• advise someone who feels sick on what to do
Types: • a description of people's vacation activities • a conversation about the previous weekend's weather **Comprehension Skill:** • focus attention	• Game (reinforces asking questions in past tense) • Writing: statements about classmates' past actions	• talk about your own weekend and vacation activities
Types: • a conversation about future activities • a phone conversation **Comprehension Skills:** • focus attention • determine context	• Game (reinforces future with *be going to*) • Reading: a postcard • Writing: a postcard	• talk about your real future plans

Acknowledgments

The authors and series director wish to acknowledge with gratitude the following consultants, reviewers, and piloters—our partners in the development of *True Colors*.

Basic Level Consultants Lucia Adrian, EF Language Schools, Miami, Florida, USA • **Martin T. Bickerstaff,** ELS Language Centers, Oakland, California, USA • **Mary C. Black,** Institute of North American Studies, Barcelona, Spain • **Amy Chang,** Chung University, Hsin Chu City, Taiwan • **Greg Conquest,** Yokohama Gaigo Business College, Japan • **George Coyle,** Chodang University, Korea • **Miles Craven,** Nihon University, Shizuoka, Japan • **Michael Davidson,** EF Language Schools, Miami, Florida, USA • **Patricia Escalante Aruaz,** Universidad de Costa Rica, San Pedro de Montes de Oca, Costa Rica • **Christina Gitsaki,** Nagoya University of Commerce and Business Administration, Japan • **John Hawkes,** EF International School, Santa Barbara, California, USA • **Susan Hills,** EF International School of English, San Diego, California, USA • **Myung-Hye Huh,** Korea University, Seoul, Korea • **Jan Kelley,** EF International School, Santa Barbara, California, USA • **Neil McClelland,** Shimonoseki City University, Japan • **Angelita Oliveira Moreno,** ICBEU, Belo Horizonte, Brazil • **Akiko Nakazawa,** Yokohama Gaigo Business College, Japan • **Esther Oliveros,** Universidad Ricardo Palma, Lima, Peru • **Ana María Orué,** Colegio América-Callao, Lima, Peru • **Ciaran Quinn,** Otemae College, Osaka, Japan • **Cecilia Rodríguez,** Universidad Ricardo Palma, Lima, Peru • **María Inés Sandoval Astudillo,** Instituto Chileno Norteamericano, Chillán, Chile • **Tatiana Suárez,** Politécnico Grancolombiano, Santafé de Bogotá, Colombia • **Yoshihiro Uzawa,** Sankei International College, Tokyo, Japan • **Martha de Vargas,** Universidad de los Andes, Santafé de Bogotá, Colombia • **Hye-bae Yoo,** University of Inchon, Korea

Course Consultants Berta de Llano, Puebla, Mexico • **Irma K. Ghosn,** Lebanese American University, Byblos, Lebanon • **Luis Fernando Gómez J.,** School of Education, University of Antioquia, Colombia • **Annie Hu,** Fu-Jen Catholic University, Taipei, Taiwan • **Nancy Lake,** CEL-LEP, São Paulo, Brazil • **Frank Lambert,** Pagoda Foreign Language Institute, Seoul, Korea • **Kazuhiko Yoshida,** Kobe University, Kobe City, Japan

Reviewers and Piloters Ronald Aviles, Instituto Chileno Norteamericano, Chuquicamata, Chile • **Liliana Baltra,** Instituto Chileno Norteamericano, Santiago, Chile • **Paulo Roberto Berkelmans,** CEL-LEP, São Paulo, Brazil • **Luis Beze,** Casa Thomas Jefferson, Brasília, Brazil • **James Boyd,** ECC Foreign Language Institute, Osaka, Japan • **Susan Bryan de Martínez,** Instituto Mexicano Norteamericano, Monterrey, Mexico • **Hugo A. Buitano,** Instituto Chileno Norteamericano, Arica, Chile • **Gary Butzbach,** American Language Center, Rabat, Morocco • **Herlinda Canto,** Universidad Popular Autónoma del Estado de Puebla, Mexico • **Rigoberto Castillo,** Colegio de CAFAM, Santafé de Bogotá, Colombia • **Tina M. Castillo,** Santafé de Bogotá, Colombia • **Amparo Clavijo Olarte,** Universidad Distrital, Santafé de Bogotá, Colombia • **Graciela Conocente,** Asociación Mendocina de Intercambio Cultural Argentino Norteamerica, Argentina • **Eduardo Corbo,** IETI, Salto, Uruguay • **Marilia Costa,** Instituto Brasil-Estados Unidos, Rio de Janeiro, Brazil • **Celia de Juan,** UNICO, UAG, Guadalajara, Mexico • **Laura de Marín,** Centro Colombo Americano, Medellín, Colombia • **Montserrat Muntaner Djmal,** Instituto Brasil-Estados Unidos, Rio de Janeiro, Brazil • **Deborah Donnelley de García,** ITESM-Campus Querétaro, Mexico • **Rosa Erlichman,** União Cultural, São Paulo, Brazil • **Guadalupe Espinoza,** ITESM-Campus Querétaro, Mexico • **Suad Farkouh,** ESL Consultant to Philadelphia National Schools, Amman, Jordan • **Niura R. H. Ferreria,** Centro Cultural Brasil Estados Unidos, Guarapuava, Brazil • **Fernando Fleurquin,** Alianza Cultural Uruguay-EEUU, Montevideo, Uruguay • **Patricia Fleury,** Casa Thomas Jefferson, Brasília, Brazil • **Patricia Foncea,** Colegio Jesualdo, Santiago, Chile • **Areta Ulhana Galat,** Centro Cultural Brasil Estados Unidos, Curitiba, Brazil • **Julie Harris de Peyré,** Universidad del Valle, Guatemala • **Ruth Hassell de Hernández,** UANL, Mexico • **Rose M. Hernández,** University of Puerto Rico-Bayamón, Puerto Rico • **Mia Kim,** Kyung Hee University, Seoul, Korea • **Junko Kobayashi,** Sankei International College, Tokyo, Japan • **Gil Lancaster,** Academy Istanbul, Istanbul, Turkey • **Mónica Lobo,** Santiago, Chile • **Luz Adriana Lopera,** Centro Colombo Americano, Medellín, Colombia • **Eva Irene Loya,** ITESM-Campus Querétaro, Mexico • **Mary Maloy Lara,** Instituto John F. Kennedy, Tehuacán, Mexico • **Meire de Jesus Marion,** Associação Alumni, São Paulo, Brazil • **Juliet Marlier,** Universidad de las Américas, Puebla, Mexico • **Yolanda Martínez,** Instituto D'Amicis, Puebla, Mexico • **Regina Celia Pereira Mendes,** Instituto Brasil-Estados Unidos, Rio de Janeiro, Brazil • **Jim Miller,** Yokohama Gaigo Business College, Japan • **Fiona Montarry,** The American Language Center, Casablanca, Morocco • **Luiz Claudio Monteiro,** Casa Thomas Jefferson, Brasília, Brazil • **Ahmed Mohammad Motala,** King Fahd University of Petroleum & Minerals, Dhahran, Saudi Arabia • **William Richard Munzer,** Universidad IDEAS de Bogotá, Colombia • **Adrian Nunn,** EF International School of English, Los Angeles, California, USA • **Margarita Ordaz Mejía,** Universidad Americana de Acapulco, Mexico • **Sherry Ou,** Fu-Jen Catholic University, Taipei, Taiwan • **Thelma Jonas Péres,** Casa Thomas Jefferson, Brasília, Brazil • **Renata Philippov,** Associação Alumni, São Paulo, Brazil • **Ron Ragsdale,** Bilgi University, Istanbul, Turkey • **Luis Ramírez F.,** Instituto Norteamericano de Cultura, Concepción, Chile • **Martha Restrepo Rodríguez,** Politécnico Grancolombiano, Santafé de Bogotá, Colombia • **Irene Reyes Giordanelli,** Centro Cultural Colombo Americano, Santiago de Cali, Colombia • **Dolores Rodríguez,** CELE (Centro de Lenguas), Universidad Autónoma de Puebla, Mexico • **Idia Rodríguez,** University of Puerto Rico-Arecibo, Puerto Rico • **Eddy Rojas & teachers,** Centro de Idiomas de la P. Universidad Católica, Peru • **Ricardo Romero,** Centro Cultural Colombo Americano, Santafé de Bogotá, Colombia • **Blanca Lilia Rosales Bremont,** Universidad Americana de Acapulco, Mexico • **Marie Adele Ryan,** Associação Alumni, São Paulo, Brazil • **Nadia Sarkis,** Uniao Cultural, São Paulo, Brazil • **Andrea Seidel,** Universidad Americana de Acapulco, Mexico • **Hada Shammar,** American Language Center, Amman, Jordan • **Lai Yin Shem,** Centro Colombo Americano, Medellín, Colombia • **Maria Cristina Siqueira,** CEL-LEP, São Paulo, Brazil • **Lilian Munhoz Soares,** Centro Cultural Brasil Estados Unidos, Santos, Brazil • **Mário César de Sousa,** Instituto Brasil-Estados Unidos, Fortaleza, Brasil • **Richard Paul Taylor,** Nagoya University of Commerce and Business Administration, Japan • **David Thompson,** Instituto Mexicano Norteamericano de Relaciones Culturales, Guadalajara, Mexico • **Nilda Valdez,** Centro Cultural Salvadoreño, El Salvador • **Euclides Valencia Cepeda,** Universidad Distrital, Santafé de Bogotá, Colombia • **Ana Verde,** American Language Institute, Montevideo, Uruguay • **Andrea Zaidenberg,** Step English Language Center, Argentina

Preface

The *True Colors* Course

True Colors is a complete and articulated six-level adult or young adult course in English as a foreign language. There are two reasons why this course is entitled *True Colors:* It presents the true voice of the native speaker of American English, and it systematically teaches students to communicate in their own words—to **let their true colors shine through.**

Each *True Colors* student's book is intended to be completed in a period of 60 to 90 class hours. There are two possible beginning-level entry points: Basic or Level 1. Basic is intended for true beginners or very weak false beginners. Level 1 is designed for false beginners, and Level 5 concludes at an advanced level.

True Colors is a highly communicative international course enhanced by strong four-skills support, including an enriched listening strand and an abundance of games, info-gaps, and other interactive and productive activities. Within each unit, vocabulary, social language, grammar, and theme are woven together and ensure concentrated oral practice and production. *True Colors* takes into account different learning and teaching styles. It incorporates task-based strategies and is centered on the well-known fact that practice in each skill area enhances mastery of the others.

True Colors is specifically designed for use by students who rarely encounter English outside of class. The course is built around a wealth of natural speaking and reading models of the true voice of the American speaker. This refreshing change from "textbook English" is essential for students who have limited access to real native speech and writing.

Because international students do not have the opportunity to talk with native speakers on a regular basis, *True Colors* does not present activities such as interviewing native speakers or watching TV in English. Instead, the course serves as a replacement for immersion in an English-speaking environment, making the classroom itself a microcosm of the English-speaking world. The goal and promise of *True Colors* is to make students comfortable understanding natural speech and competent at speaking, reading, and writing real English at each level.

Research

The *True Colors* course has been pilot-tested and reviewed by educators throughout the world and used by students of numerous language groups. The finished course represents the contributions of this substantial research.

True Colors Basic Level

Focus and Approach *True Colors* Basic provides a beginning-level entry point for true beginners or very weak false beginners. It stresses thematic vocabulary development, elementary social language, and basic, beginning-level grammar. The goal of *True*

Colors Basic is to bring the student to a false-beginner level in a short period of time. The student completing *True Colors* Basic will be ready for *True Colors* Level 1.

An important innovation of *True Colors* Basic is to systematically build students' vocabularies, integrating all new words with social language and simple yet essential grammar so that students quickly begin to communicate, even within the limited goals of the true beginner. Two major goals of all the *True Colors* texts are enabling students to express their own ideas, opinions, and feelings and helping them to improvise with language they learn in class. To this end, each unit of *True Colors* Basic includes two unique activities, **Improvise** and **In Your Own Words**, which ready beginning students for improvisation and personal expression.

True beginners cannot be expected to bring previously taught language with them to the classroom. For this reason, vocabulary and grammar are strictly controlled and continually reentered and recombined for successful mastery and rapid progress. Except for the **Listening with a Purpose** listening texts (see page ix), all language within each student's book unit is at students' productive level so they will feel successful and competent at every language activity.

Components of *True Colors* Basic

Although the student's book is a complete teaching tool in itself, giving presentation, practice, and production of all four skills, a full complement of supplementary materials is available to further support the material.

Student's Book The student's book is made up of ten units and two review units, one coming after Unit 5 and the other after Unit 10.

Teacher's Edition The teacher's edition is interleaved with full-color student's book pages and contains an introduction to the format and approach of *True Colors;* page-by-page teaching suggestions especially written for the teacher who teaches outside an English-speaking country; tapescripts for the audiocassettes or audio CDs; and a complete answer key to the exercises in the student's book and workbook and to the achievement tests.

Teacher's Bonus Pack The Teacher's Bonus Pack is a unique set of reproducible hands-on learning-support activities that includes flashcards for large- or small-group vocabulary presentations, duplicating masters of full-page illustrations with empty speech balloons for student oral and written discussion, learner-completed grammar boxes, and two kinds of interactive conversation cards—one for social language reinforcement and one for expansion and oral review.

Workbook The workbook contains numerous additional yet highly controlled opportunities for written reinforcement of the language taught in the student's book. The exercises in the workbook are suitable for homework or classwork.

Audiocassettes or Audio CDs The audiocassettes or audio CDs contain all the vocabulary presentations, the conversations, and all exercises that could be recorded. They also contain the Listening with a Purpose skills-based listening texts. The cassettes and CDs provide space for student practice and self-correction.

Achievement Tests Achievement tests offer opportunities for evaluation of student progress on a unit-by-unit basis. In addition, a midterm and a final test are provided.

Videocassette The videocassette, *True Voices,* contains a unique combination of unit-by-unit controlled conversations to reinforce the social language and grammar taught in the *True Colors* Basic student's book, visual vocabulary presentations to activate vocabulary use, and short, personal, on-the-street interviews to help build students' comprehension of authentic language at a slightly higher, or receptive, level.

Video Workbook A video workbook enhances listening comprehension and provides active language practice and reinforcement of all vocabulary, social language, and grammar from the video.

Vocabulary

Captioned Illustrations The meaning of each unit's new vocabulary is clearly conveyed by captioned illustrations. These words form the core of the unit's vocabulary and will reappear in each later part of the unit.

In Your Own Words Short, focused activities follow and provide students an opportunity to use the new words in sentences and phrases of their own. A clear example serves as a model for this activity.

Practice This exercise provides controlled practice of the new vocabulary.

Social Language and Grammar Social language and grammar are linked in a series of two to four short lessons consisting of the following elements:

Conversation A short dialogue presents and models important social language and strategies for productive use.

Grammar Clear grammar presentations support comprehension and expression of the social language from the conversation. These grammar presentations never occur in isolation; rather, they form a support for the social language of the lesson, giving the grammar both meaning and purpose. To this end, grammar exercises are set in a context that supports the communicative focus of the lesson.

Pair Practice The conversation is presented again for further student practice, this time with opportunities for personalization of the social language. This controlled opportunity for manipulation is the first step toward ownership of the language, which is the goal and promise of *True Colors.*

Improvise An important aim of *True Colors* is to teach students to improvise with the language they already know. Improvisation is the "fifth skill"—the strategy students need to master in order to move out of the pages of a textbook and into the real world.

Listening with a Purpose Listening with a Purpose accustoms Basic students to receptive-level language—language slightly above their own productive ability. The two-step comprehension syllabus centers on two essential listening strategies—determining context and focusing attention. Through a unique approach to listening comprehension incorporating skills similar to the reading comprehension skills of skimming and scanning, students make significant progress toward understanding real English.

Expansion Activities Each unit contains at least one additional reading, writing, oral-interactive activity, or game that recombines, activates, reinforces, and integrates the vocabulary, grammar, and social language of that unit and of previous units.

 This unique full-page illustration has been carefully designed to elicit from students all the language they have learned in the unit—the vocabulary, the social language, the grammar, and the thematic contexts. Students ask each other questions about the actions depicted, make true and false statements about what they see, create conversations for the characters, and tell stories about what is happening—all IN THEIR OWN WORDS. All students, regardless of ability, will succeed at their own levels because what they know how to say has been drawn into the illustration and what they don't know how to say has been purposely left out. Furthermore, because language learning is a process of continuing activation, the In Your Own Words illustrations include opportunities to recycle and reuse vocabulary, grammar, and social language from previous units as well.

Review Units There are two review units: one after Unit 5 (midbook) and the other at the end, after Unit 10. They provide review, general self-tests, extra classroom practice, and a special social language self-test, all designed to reinforce new language on a cumulative basis.

About the Authors and Series Director

Authors

Jay Maurer

Jay Maurer has taught English at binational centers, colleges, and universities in Portugal, Spain, Mexico, the Somali Republic, and the United States. In addition, he taught intensive English at Columbia University's American Language Program.

Dr. Maurer has an M.A. and an M.Ed. in Applied Linguistics as well as a Ph.D. in The Teaching of English, all from Columbia University. In addition to this new adult and young adult English course, he is the author of the Advanced Level of Longman's widely acclaimed *Focus on Grammar* series and coauthor of the three-level *Structure Practice in Context* series and coauthor of the *True Voices* video series. Dr. Maurer teaches and writes in the Seattle, Washington, area and recently conducted a series of teaching workshops in Brazil and Japan.

Irene E. Schoenberg

Irene E. Schoenberg has taught English to international students for over twenty years at Hunter College's International Language Institute and at Columbia University's American Language Program. Additionally, she trains English instructors in EFL/ESL teaching methods at The New School for Social Research. Her M.A. is in TESOL from Columbia University. She is a popular speaker to national and international TESOL groups.

Professor Schoenberg is the author of the Basic Level of the *Focus on Grammar* series as well as two engaging, unique, and widely used conversation texts, *Talk About Trivia* and *Talk About Values*. In addition to *True Colors*, Professor Schoenberg coauthored the *True Voices* video series.

Series Director

Joan Saslow

Joan Saslow has taught English and foreign languages to adults and young adults in both South America and the United States. She taught English at the binational centers of Valparaíso and Viña del Mar, Chile, and English and French at the Catholic University of Valparaíso. She taught English to Japanese university students at Marymount College and to international students in Westchester Community College's intensive program.

Ms. Saslow, whose B.A. and M.A. are from the University of Wisconsin, is author of *English in Context: Reading Comprehension for Science and Technology,* a three-level series. In addition, she has been an editor of language-teaching materials, a teacher trainer, and a frequent speaker at gatherings of English teachers outside the United States for over twenty-five years.

 # Welcome.

VOCABULARY 🎧

listen

speak

read

write

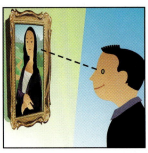
look

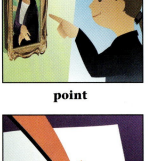
point

circle

complete

a letter

a word

a sentence

a question

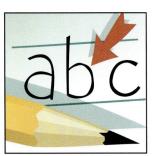
a book

a class

a partner   a partner

a picture

DIRECTIONS

Listen to the conversation.

Hi. I'm Sally.

Hi, Sally. My name is Tom.

Practice the conversation with a partner.

Hi. I'm Anne.

Hi, Anne. My name is Jim.

Ask a question.

What's your name?

Answer the question.

Jim.

Write your name.

Talk about the picture with a partner.

Conversation

🎧 *Listen and read.*

🎧 *Listen again and practice.*

Pair Practice

Practice with a partner. Use your own name.

A: Hello. I'm _____.

B: Hi, _____. I'm _____.

A: Nice to meet you, _____.

B: Nice to meet you too.

SOCIAL LANGUAGE 2

Conversation

🎧 *Listen and read.*

John, this is Adam. Adam, this is John.

Hi, Adam. Nice to meet you.

Nice to meet you too.

🎧 *Listen again and practice.*

Pair Practice

Practice with two partners. Use your own words.

A: _____, this is _____. _____, this is _____.

B: Hi, _____. Nice to meet you.

C: Nice to meet you too.

 Look at these pictures. Create conversations. Use your own words.

I'm a student.

PEOPLE AND OCCUPATIONS

VOCABULARY

Occupations

🎧 *Look at the pictures. Listen. Say each word.*

a student   a teacher

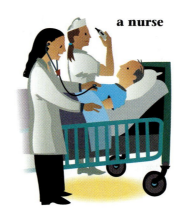

a nurse

a doctor

a writer

a singer

a homemaker

a businessman   a businesswoman

In Your Own Words

With a partner, talk about a picture. Point. Use your own words.

Examples: She's a student.

He's a writer.

Practice 1

🎧 *Listen and point.*

Practice 2

*Practice with a partner. Look at **Practice 1**.*
Partner A, say an occupation.
Partner B, point to the picture.

Example: a singer

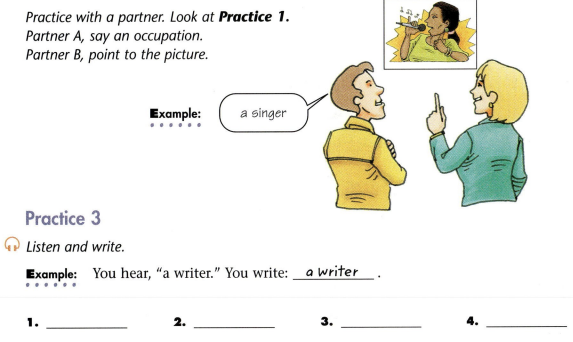

Practice 3

🎧 *Listen and write.*

Example: You hear, "a writer." You write: __a writer__ .

1. _____   2. _____   3. _____   4. _____

More Occupations

🎧 *Look at the pictures. Listen. Say each word.*

an artist   **an actor**   **an engineer**   **an athlete**

 With a partner, talk about a picture. Use your own words.

Example: He's an artist.

Practice

Look at the pictures. Write the occupations.

Example:

a singer

1. _____   **2.** _____   **3.** _____   **4.** _____

🎧 *Now listen and check your work.*

The Alphabet

🎧 *Look at the letters. Listen. Say each letter.*

A a   B b   C c   D d   E e   F f   G g   H h   I i   J j   K k   L l   M m
N n   O o   P p   Q q   R r   S s   T t   U u   V v   W w   X x   Y y   Z z

Practice

🎧 *Listen and circle.*

1. a   e   i   j   **2.** u   w   o   q   **3.** g   j   z   y   **4.** f   v   b   w

Receptive Model

LISTENING WITH A PURPOSE

🎧 *Look at the names. Listen.*

1. **a.** A – L – L – A – N   **b.** A – L – A – N   **c.** A – L – L – E – N

2. **a.** W – I – N – E   **b.** W – Y – N – E   **c.** W – E – I – N

3. **a.** L – Y – N – N   **b.** L – Y – N   **c.** L – I – N – N

4. **a.** G – R – E – E – N – E   **b.** G – R – E – E – N   **c.** G – R – E – N – E

🎧 *Now listen again. Circle the correct name.*

SOCIAL LANGUAGE AND GRAMMAR   1

Conversation 1

🎧 *Listen and read.*

A: Are you Elaine?
B: Yes, I am.

🎧 *Listen again and practice.*

Conversation 2

🎧 *Listen and read.*

A: Are you Barry?
B: No, I'm not. I'm Jack.

🎧 *Listen again and practice.*

Pair Practice

Practice with a partner. Use your own words.

A: Are you _____?

B: _____.

Verb **Be**: Statements		
full form		**contractions**
I **am** a teacher.	=	**I'm** a teacher.
You **are** a student.	=	**You're** a student.
He **is** a doctor.	=	**He's** a doctor.
She **is** a businesswoman.	=	**She's** a businesswoman.
Mary **is** a nurse.	=	**Mary's** a nurse.

Grammar Practice

Complete the sentences.

Example:

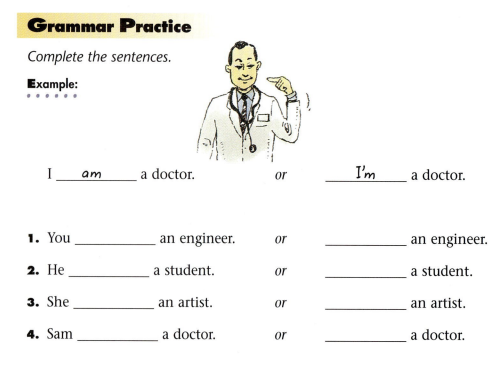

I ___*am*___ a doctor.   *or*   ___*I'm*___ a doctor.

1. You _____ an engineer.   *or*   _____ an engineer.

2. He _____ a student.   *or*   _____ a student.

3. She _____ an artist.   *or*   _____ an artist.

4. Sam _____ a doctor.   *or*   _____ a doctor.

SOCIAL LANGUAGE AND GRAMMAR 2

Be: Yes-No Questions and Short Answers		
questions	**affirmative answers**	**negative answers**
Are you a student?	Yes, I am.	No, I'm not.
Is he a doctor?	Yes, he is.	No, he's not. (or No, he isn't.)
Is she an athlete?	Yes, she is.	No, she's not. (or No, she isn't.)

Grammar Practice

Look at the pictures. Answer the questions.

Example: **A:** Is he an artist?   **A:** Is she a doctor?   **A:** Is he an actor?

B: ___Yes, he is___ .   **B:** _____ .   **B:** _____ .

Conversation 1

🎧 *Listen and read.*

A: Is he a doctor?
B: No, he's not. He's a businessman.

🎧 *Listen again and practice.*

Conversation 2

🎧 *Listen and read.*

A: Is Janet a teacher?
B: Yes, she is.

🎧 *Listen again and practice.*

Pair Practice

*Practice with a partner. Look at **In Your Own Words** on page 13. Point. Ask about occupations. Use your own words.*

Examples:　**A:** Is he an athlete?
　　　　　　　B: No, he's not. He's a doctor.

Improvise

Talk to a partner.
Talk about your occupation.

Conversation 3

🎧 *Listen and read.*

A: What do you do, Alex?
B: I'm a writer. What about you?
A: I'm a student.

🎧 *Listen again and practice.*

Variations

What about you?
And you?
And what do you do?

Pair Practice

Practice with a partner. Use your own words.

A: What do you do, _____?

B: _____. _____?

A: _____.

A and An	
a	**an**
*a t*eacher	*an* artist
*a d*octor	*an* engineer

Grammar Practice

*Write **a** or **an**.*

Example: I'm _____*a*_____ doctor.

1. I'm _____ artist.

2. You're _____ businessman.

3. You're _____ singer.

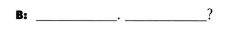

LISTENING WITH A PURPOSE

🎧 *Look at the chart. Listen.*

NAME:	Amy Browne
OCCUPATION:	
NAME:	Bart
OCCUPATION:	

🎧 *Now listen again. Complete the chart.*

Are You _____?

Work with a partner. Write names in the chart.

Name	Occupation
Shakespeare	writer
Pelé	athlete
	teacher
	actor
	singer
	doctor

Now practice with a partner. Choose a name and an occupation from the chart.

Example:
A: Are you an actor?
B: No, I'm not.
A: Are you a writer?
B: Yes, I am.
A: Are you Shakespeare?
B: Yes, I am.

Now play as a class. Make cards with names from the chart.

Tape a card on a classmate's back. Look at the pictures.

Ask the class about the card on your back.

- Point and name the occupations.
  Example: *He's a businessman.*
- Ask your partner **yes-no** questions.
  Example: *Is she Anne?*
- Answer questions.
  Example: *Yes, she is.*
- Create conversations for the people.
  Example: A: *John, is that J-O-H-N?*
  B: *No, it's J-O-N.*

13

Who are they?

PEOPLE AND FAMILIES

VOCABULARY

Adjectives

🎧 *Look at the pictures. Listen. Say each word.*

married **single**   **young** **old**

tall   **short**   **good**   **bad**

With a partner, talk about a picture. Point. Ask and answer a question.
Use your own words.

Example: **A:** Is he married?
　　　　　　　B: Yes, he is.

Who are they?

My sister and her two friends.

Are they single?

No. They're married.

Practice

Look at the pictures. Listen. Number the pictures 1, 2, 3, and 4.

a. _____

b. _____

c. ___1___

d. _____

Male and Female

Look at the pictures. Listen. Say each word.

a man   **a woman**   **a boy**   **a girl**

Practice

Look at the pictures. Listen. Number the pictures 1, 2, 3, and 4.

a. _____

b. _____

c. _____

d. _____

Relationships

🎧 *Look at the pictures. Listen. Say each word.*

friends　　　　　　**classmates**　　　　　　**neighbors**

 With a partner, talk about a picture. Point.

Example:　They're classmates.

Practice

🎧 *Listen and write.*

Example:　You hear, "a young classmate." You write: ___*a young classmate*___.

1. _____　　2. _____　　3. _____

The Family

🎧 *Look at the pictures. Listen. Say each word.*

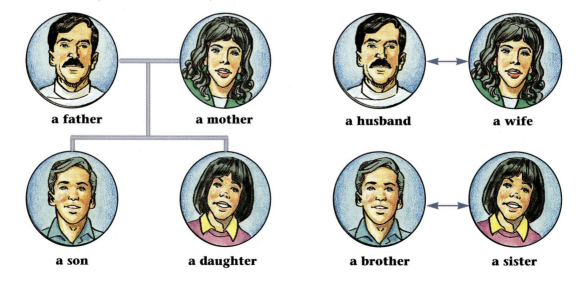

a father　　**a mother**　　　**a husband**　　**a wife**

a son　　**a daughter**　　　**a brother**　　**a sister**

Practice

Look at the pictures. Complete the sentences about the family.

Example: This is a picture of me. I'm a good student, but I'm a bad athlete.

1. This is my _____. He's a bad student, but he's a good athlete.

2. This is my _____. She's an engineer.

3. This is my _____. He's a doctor.

🎧 *Now listen and check your work.*

Numbers

🎧 *Look at the numbers. Listen. Say each number.*

1	2	3	4	5	6	7	8	9	10
one	two	three	four	five	six	seven	eight	nine	ten

LISTENING WITH A PURPOSE

🎧 *Look at the numbers. Listen.*

1. a. 662-4798   **b.** 664-4789   **2. a.** 525-8371   **b.** 552-8713

🎧 *Now listen again. Circle the correct answer.*

SOCIAL LANGUAGE AND GRAMMAR 1

Singular and Plural Nouns	
singular nouns	**plural nouns**
a *student*	*students*
a *son*	*sons*
one *man*	three *men*
one *woman*	two *women*

Grammar Practice

🎧 *Listen and write.*

Example: You hear, "two boys." You write: __two boys__ .

1. _____

2. _____

3. _____

4. _____

Be: Statements and Questions (plural)	
statements	

We *are* students.
(*or* We*'re* students.)

You *are* tall.
(*or* You*'re* tall.)

They *are* married.
(*or* They*'re* married.)

questions	**answers**
Are they married?	Yes, they are. (*not* ~~Yes, they're.~~)
Are they old?	No, they're not. (*or* No, they aren't.)

Grammar Practice

Complete the conversations. Use **we're, we are, they're,** or **they are.**

Example: **A:** Are you artists?
        B: No, ____we're____ not.

1. **A:** Are they teachers?

    B: No, _____ not. They're students.

2. **A:** Are you married?

    B: No, _____ not.

3. **A:** Are they businessmen?

    B: Yes, _____.

4. **A:** Are you good singers?

    B: Yes, _____.

Conversation

Listen and read.

A: Who are they?
B: My two friends.
A: Are they single?
B: No. They're married.

Listen again and practice.

Pair Practice

Practice with a partner. Use your own words.

A: Who are they?

B: My _____.

A: Are they _____?

B: _____.

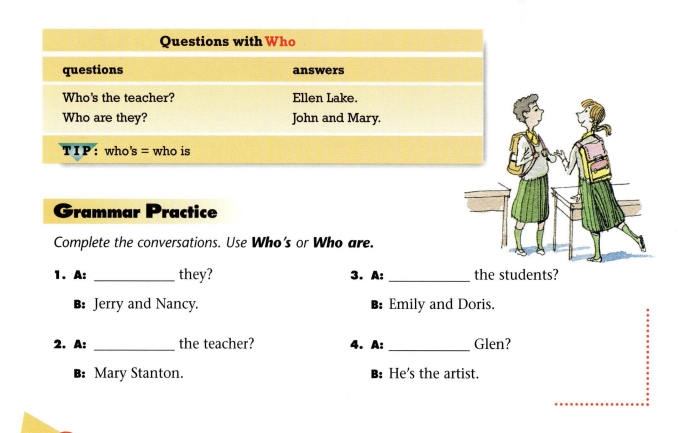

Questions with Who	
questions	answers
Who's the teacher?	Ellen Lake.
Who are they?	John and Mary.

TIP: who's = who is

Grammar Practice

*Complete the conversations. Use **Who's** or **Who are.***

1. A: _____ they?

B: Jerry and Nancy.

2. A: _____ the teacher?

B: Mary Stanton.

3. A: _____ the students?

B: Emily and Doris.

4. A: _____ Glen?

B: He's the artist.

SOCIAL LANGUAGE AND GRAMMAR 2

Possessive Adjectives			
I	my	we	our
you	your	you	your
he	his	they	their
she	her		

his sister   *her* brother

Grammar Practice

Complete the conversations.

Example: **A:** Is this her father?

B: No. He's ___*her*___ friend.

her / your

1. A: Is this your sister?

B: No. She's _____ daughter.

your / my

2. A: Is this his mother?

B: No. She's _____ wife.

his / her

3. A: Are these your brothers?

B: No. They're _____ sons!

my / your

Conversation

🎧 *Listen and read.*

A: Hello, Jim.

B: Oh, hi, Anne. How's it going?

A: Great.

B: Anne, this is my brother Ray.

A: Hi, Ray.

C: Hi.

B: And this is his friend Steve.

A: Hi, Steve.

D: Hi.

🎧 *Listen again and practice.*

Variations

How's it going?
How are you?
How are you doing?

Variations

Great.
OK.
Fine, thanks.

Pair Practice

Practice with three partners.
Use your own words.

A: Hello, _____.

B: Oh, hi, _____. How _____?

A: _____.

B: _____, this is my _____ _____.

A: Hi, _____.

C: Hi.

B: And this is _____ _____ _____.

A: Hi, _____.

D: Hi.

SOCIAL LANGUAGE AND GRAMMAR 3

Conversation

🎧 *Listen and read.*

A: What's your name?
B: Art Stein.
A: OK. And what's your phone number?
B: 478-9803.
A: 478-9830?
B: No. 478-9803.
A: Oh. OK, thanks.
B: You're welcome.

🎧 *Listen again and practice.*

Variations

Thanks.
Thanks a lot.
Thank you.

Pair Practice

Practice with a partner. Use your own words.

A: What's your name?

B: _____.

A: OK. And what's your phone number?

B: _____.

A: _____?

B: No. _____.

A: Oh. OK, _____.

B: _____.

Questions with **What**	
questions	**answers**
What's his name?	John Williams.
What's their phone number?	280-9763.

TIP: what's = what is

Grammar with a Partner

Ask your partner a question. Write the answer.

Examples: What's your name?
What's your phone number?

Grammar Practice

*Complete the conversations. Use **Who's** or **What's**.*

1. A: _____ the doctor?

   B: Marsha Gordon.

2. A: _____ her phone number?

   B: 778-2114.

3. A: _____ her husband?

   B: Carl Gordon.

4. A: _____ his phone number?

   B: It's 778-2114, too.

Improvise

Look at a photo of your family or friends.
Talk with a partner.
Ask and answer questions.

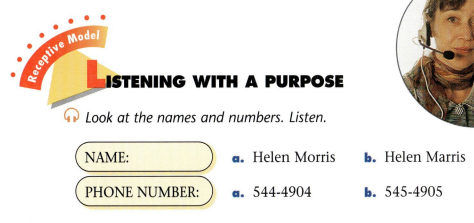

Receptive Model

LISTENING WITH A PURPOSE

🎧 *Look at the names and numbers. Listen.*

| NAME: | **a.** Helen Morris | **b.** Helen Marris | **c.** Helen Maurice |

| PHONE NUMBER: | **a.** 544-4904 | **b.** 545-4905 | **c.** 544-4905 |

🎧 *Now listen again. Circle the correct answer.*

Listening Bingo

🎧 *Listen. Circle the letters you hear. Find a word.*

1	2	3	4	5	6
f	z	b	f	L	b
c	(r)	y	a	d	x
r	p	i	d	g	a
a	L	c	e	u	r
i	e	t	w	n	u
n	s	e	r	s	d

What is the word?

____ ____ ____ ____ ____

Guess the Truth

Play in groups of four. Each student writes three true statements and two false statements. Read your statements. Each student guesses "true" or "false."

My husband is an actor. True or false?

False.

True.

False.

In **Your** Own **Words**

- Point and talk about the people.
  Example: *They're married.*

- Ask and answer questions with **what**.
  Example: *A: What's her phone number?*

- Ask and answer questions with **who**.
  Example: *A: Who's the boy?*
  B: He's her brother.

- Create conversations for the people.
  Example: *A: What's your phone number?*
  B: 232-1748.

232-1748

Unit 3

Where is Bob?

PLACES AND THINGS

VOCABULARY

Places

🎧 *Look at the picture. Listen. Say each word or phrase.*

**the bank   the supermarket   the gym   the post office   the library   the theater
the stadium   the hospital**

With a partner, talk about the picture. Use your own words.

Example: The library is on Oak Avenue.

Practice

Look back at **Places**. *Complete the sentences.*

Example: ___The post office___ is on Oak Avenue.
<u>The bank / The post office</u>

1. _____ is on
<u>The theater / The gym</u>
Main Street.

2. _____ is on
<u>The supermarket / The library</u>
Oak Avenue.

3. _____ is on
<u>The bank / The gym</u>
Oak Avenue.

🎧 *Now listen and check your work.*

Places We Live

🎧 *Look at the picture. Listen. Say each word.*

In Your Own Words

With a partner, talk about the picture. Use your own words.

Example: The apartment is on Maple Street.

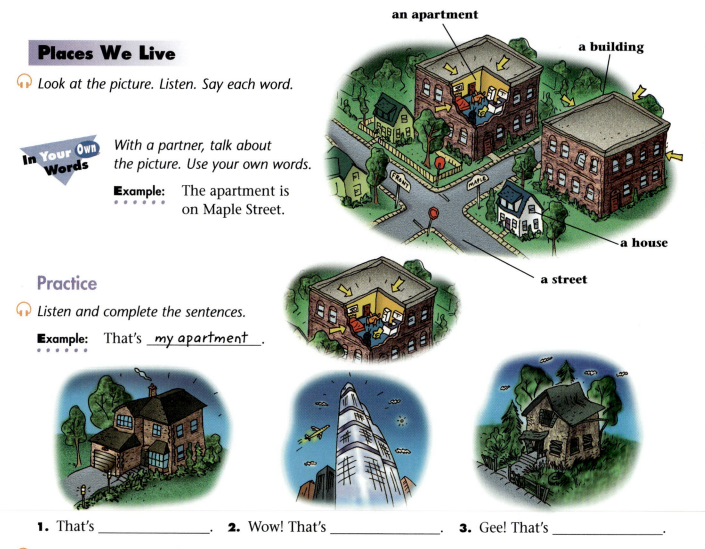

an apartment

a building

a house

a street

Practice

🎧 *Listen and complete the sentences.*

Example: That's ___my apartment___.

1. That's _____. **2.** Wow! That's _____. **3.** Gee! That's _____.

🎧 *Now listen again and check your work.*

Adjectives

🎧 *Look at the picture. Listen. Say each word.*

beautiful

small

big

new

ugly

$15000.00

expensive

cheap

$25.00

In Your Own Words

With a partner, talk about the pictures. Point. Use your own words.

Example: That's an ugly picture.

Practice

🎧 *Look at the pictures. Listen. Number the pictures 1, 2, 3, and 4.*

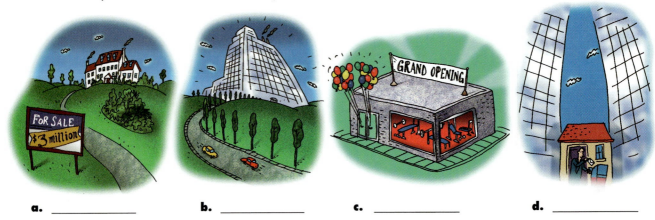

FOR SALE
$3 million

GRAND OPENING

a. _____ b. _____ c. _____ d. _____

Personal Items

🎧 *Look at the pictures. Listen. Say each word.*

a watch
The watch is from Japan.*

a ring
The ring is from Mexico.

a belt
The belt is from Brazil.

a briefcase
The briefcase is from Korea.

a purse
The purse is from France.

a wallet
The wallet is from Italy.

*See pages 136–137 for place names.

In Your Own Words

With a partner, talk about your personal items. Use your own words.

Example: My watch is from France.

Practice

Match the pictures and the phrases.

1. a cheap belt _____c_____

2. a beautiful ring _____

3. an expensive wallet _____

4. a new watch _____

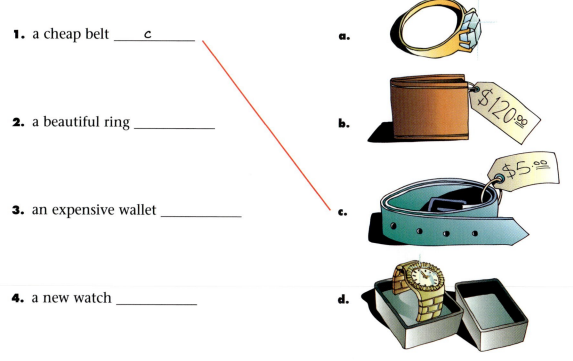

a.

b. $120.⁰⁰

c. $5.⁰⁰

d.

🎧 *Look at the numbers. Listen. Say each number.*

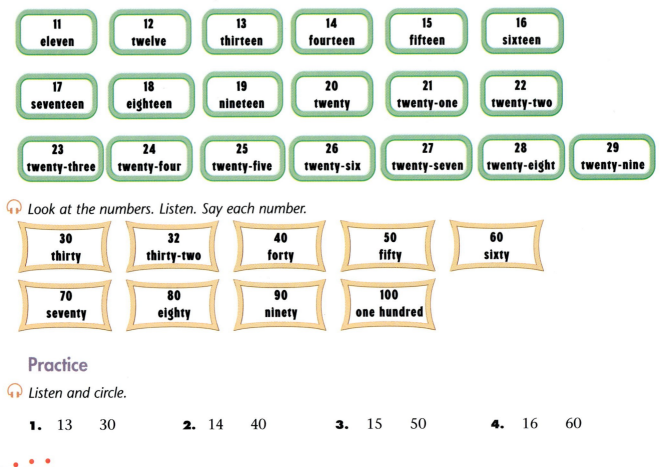

11 eleven	12 twelve	13 thirteen	14 fourteen	15 fifteen	16 sixteen
17 seventeen	18 eighteen	19 nineteen	20 twenty	21 twenty-one	22 twenty-two
23 twenty-three	24 twenty-four	25 twenty-five	26 twenty-six	27 twenty-seven	28 twenty-eight	29 twenty-nine

🎧 *Look at the numbers. Listen. Say each number.*

| 30 thirty | 32 thirty-two | 40 forty | 50 fifty | 60 sixty |
| 70 seventy | 80 eighty | 90 ninety | 100 one hundred |

Practice

🎧 *Listen and circle.*

1. 13   30   **2.** 14   40   **3.** 15   50   **4.** 16   60

Receptive Model

LISTENING WITH A PURPOSE

🎧 *Listen to the addresses.*

🎧 *Listen again. Check (√) the addresses you hear.*

Example: ☑ 15 Oak Avenue
☐ 50 Oak Avenue

1. ☐ 13 Main Street
☐ 30 Main Street

2. ☐ 17 Smith Avenue
☐ 70 Smith Avenue

3. ☐ 18 Avenue A
☐ 80 Avenue A

SOCIAL LANGUAGE AND GRAMMAR 1

Questions with Where	
questions	**answers**
Where is she?	At the supermarket.
Where are you?	We're at the bank.
Where's the post office?	On Oak Avenue.

TIP: where's = where is

Grammar Practice 1

Complete the conversations.

Example: **A:** Where ___*is he*___ ?

B: He's at the post office.

1. A: Where _____?

B: They're at the supermarket.

2. A: Where _____?

B: I'm in the hospital.

3. A: Where _____?

B: We're on Market Street.

4. A: Where _____ Mary?

B: She's at the gym.

Grammar Practice 2

Write the sentences with contractions.

Example: Where is Ken? _____*Where's Ken*_____ ?

1. Where is the bank? _____?

2. Where is the gym? _____?

Conversation

🎧 *Listen and read.*

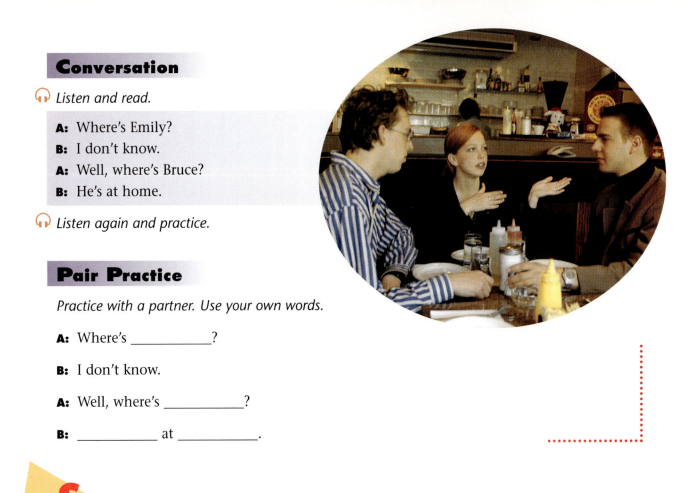

A: Where's Emily?
B: I don't know.
A: Well, where's Bruce?
B: He's at home.

🎧 *Listen again and practice.*

Pair Practice

Practice with a partner. Use your own words.

A: Where's _____?

B: I don't know.

A: Well, where's _____?

B: _____ at _____.

SOCIAL LANGUAGE AND GRAMMAR 2

It	
question	answer
Where's the bank?	*It is* on Main Street. = *It's* on Main Street.

Grammar Practice

*Complete the conversations. Use **He's, She's,** or **It's.***

Example: **A:** Where's your brother?
B: _____He's_____ at home.

1. A: Where's your sister?

B: _____ at home.

2. A: Where's the library?

B: _____ on Park Street.

3. A: Where's your father?

B: _____ at work.

4. A: Where's the post office?

B: _____ on State Street.

Conversation

🎧 *Listen and read.*

A: Where's the house?
B: It's on Main Street.
A: Oh. What's the address?
B: Twelve Main Street.

🎧 *Listen again and practice.*

Pair Practice

Practice with a partner. Use your own words.

A: Where's _____?

B: It's on _____.

A: Oh. What's the address?

B: _____.

Improvise

Work with a partner.
Talk about places where you live.
Ask and answer questions.

SOCIAL LANGUAGE AND GRAMMAR 3

Not
She's *not* at home. She's at school.
Are they from Panama?   No, they're *not* from Panama. They're from Peru.

Grammar Practice

*Complete the negative statements. Use **not**.*

Example: Nina ___*is not*___ here. She's at the movies.

1. His watch _____ from Japan. It's from Mexico.

2. They _____ at work. They're at school.

Conversation

🎧 *Listen and read.*

A: That's a beautiful belt!
B: Oh, thanks a lot.
A: Where's it from? Brazil?
B: No, it's not. It's from Italy.

🎧 *Listen again and practice.*

Variations

That's a beautiful belt!
That's a nice belt.
What a beautiful belt!

Pair Practice

Practice with a partner. Use your own words.

A: That's a beautiful _____!

B: Oh, _____.

A: Where's it from? _____?

B: No, _____. _____.

 **Improvise**

Talk to a classmate about a personal item.

LISTENING WITH A PURPOSE

🎧 *Read the statements. Listen to the conversation.*

	True	False	I don't know.
1. The teacher is Mr. Salvo.	☐	☑	☐
2. He is from Houston.	☐	☐	☐
3. He is their new teacher.	☐	☐	☐
4. He is a good teacher.	☐	☐	☐

🎧 *Now listen again. Check (√) **true, false,** or **I don't know.***

Expansion Game — Personal Items

Check (√) your personal items on the chart.

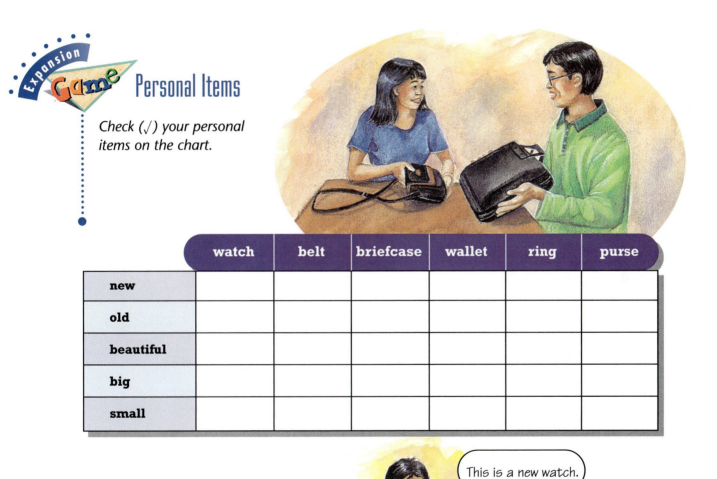

	watch	belt	briefcase	wallet	ring	purse
new						
old						
beautiful						
big						
small						

Tell a partner about your personal items.

This is a new watch.

READING AND WRITING
Business Cards

Read the business cards.
Ask a partner questions.

Example:　Where's Paul Chen from?
　　　　　　What's his address?
　　　　　　Is he an engineer?

Partner A, ask questions about Antonio Blanca.
Partner B, ask questions about Amy Wilson.

Answer the questions.

Now make your own business card.

- With a partner, talk about people and places.
  Example: *Antonio is short.*
  The post office is small.

- Ask and answer questions with **where, what,** and **who.**
  Example: *A: Where's Paul?*
  B: He's on Water Street.

- Create conversations for the people.
  Example: *A: Where's the post office?*
  B: It's on Water Street.

- Write five false statements. Your partner corrects the statements.
  Example: *A: The post office is on Center Street.*
  B: No, the post office is on Water Street.

When is the movie?

EVENTS AND TIME

VOCABULARY

Events

🎧 *Look at the pictures. Listen. Say each word or phrase.*

a movie   **a concert**   **a play**

a soccer game   **a basketball game**

a dance   **a party**

In Your Own Words

With a partner, talk about a picture. Point. Use your own words.

Example: There's a soccer game at the stadium.

Hello, Peter?

Yes?

This is Sara.
When's the movie?

Oh, hi, Sara.
It's at seven.

Practice

Look at the pictures. Complete the sentences.

Example: There's <u>*a soccer game*</u> at the stadium.

1. There's _____ at the theater.

2. There's _____ at the Cineplex.

3. There's _____ at the library.

4. There's _____ at my house.

🎧 *Now listen and check your work.*

Days of the Week

🎧 *Look at the calendar. Listen. Say each day.*

Monday	Friday
Tuesday	Saturday
Wednesday	Sunday
Thursday	

Monday	Tuesday	Wednesday	Thursday	Friday	Saturday	Sunday
9	10	11	12	13	14	15
concert 9 pm	play 7 pm	basketball game 3 pm	movie 8 pm	party 8 pm	soccer game 10 am	

Work with a partner. Look at the calendar. Ask and answer questions.

Example: **A:** When is the play?
B: It's on Tuesday.

Practice

🎧 *Listen to the conversations. Write the day.*

Example: You hear, "When is the concert?" "It's on Monday." You write: __Monday__.

1. _____   3. _____

2. _____   4. _____

🎧 *Now listen again and check your work.*

Time of the Day

🎧 *Look at the pictures. Listen. Say each word.*

morning   **afternoon**   **night**

 In Your Own Words   *Work with a partner. Look at the calendar on page 39. Ask and answer questions.*

Example: **A:** When is the party?
B: It's on Friday night.

Practice

🎧 *Listen and write.*

Example: You hear, "Tuesday morning." You write: _Tuesday morning_.

1. _____   2. _____   3. _____

Time Expressions

🎧 *Look at the picture. Listen. Say each word and sentence.*

today	**Today** is Wednesday.
tonight	There's a party **tonight**.
tomorrow	**Tomorrow** is Thursday.

Wednesday

9:00 am	
10:00	
11:00	
12:00 pm	
1:00	
2:00	
3:00	
4:00	
5:00	
6:00	
7:00	
8:00	Party

Practice

*Complete the sentences. Use **today**, **tonight**, and **tomorrow**.*

Example: ___Today___ is Friday.

1. There's a concert _____.

2. There's a basketball game _____.

3. _____ is Saturday.

🎧 *Now listen and check your work.*

Friday

9:00 am	
10:00	
11:00	
12:00 pm	
1:00	Basketball Game
2:00	
3:00	
4:00	
5:00	
6:00	
6:30	
7:00	
7:30	Concert
8:00	
8:30	
9:00	

Telling Time

🎧 *Look at the pictures. Listen. Say each phrase.*

 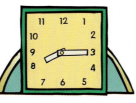  

| **eight o'clock** (8:00) | **eight-fifteen** (8:15) | **eight-thirty** (8:30) | **eight forty-five** (8:45) |

In Your Own Words

With a partner, talk about a picture. Point. Ask and answer questions.

Example: **A:** What time is it?
B: It's eight o'clock.

Practice 1

Practice with a partner. Partner A says the time. Partner B points.
Then, Partner B says the time. Partner A points.

Example:

seven forty-five

Practice 2

Say each time.

Example: 8:00
You say, "It's eight o'clock."

1. 6:00   **2.** 5:15   **3.** 4:30   **4.** 12:45

🎧 *Now listen and check your work.*

Months of the Year

🎧 *Look at the calendars. Listen. Say each month.*

January
February
March
April
May
June
July
August
September
October
November
December

January						
M	T	W	T	F	S	S
	1	2	3	4	5	6
7	8	9	10	11	12	13
14	15	16	17	18	19	20
21	22	23	24	25	26	27
28	29	30	31			

February						
M	T	W	T	F	S	S
				1	2	3
4	5	6	7	8	9	10
11	12	13	14	15	16	17
18	19	20	21	22	23	24
25	26	27	28			

March						
M	T	W	T	F	S	S
				1	2	3
4	5	6	7	8	9	10
11	12	13	14	15	16	17
18	19	20	21	22	23	24
25	26	27	28	29	30	31

April						
M	T	W	T	F	S	S
1	2	3	4	5	6	7
8	9	10	11	12	13	14
15	16	17	18	19	20	21
22	23	24	25	26	27	28
29	30					

May						
M	T	W	T	F	S	S
	1	2	3	4	5	
6	7	8	9	10	11	12
13	14	15	16	17	18	19
20	21	22	23	24	25	26
27	28	29	30	31		

June						
M	T	W	T	F	S	S
					1	2
3	4	5	6	7	8	9
10	11	12	13	14	15	16
17	18	19	20	21	22	23
24	25	26	27	28	29	30

July						
M	T	W	T	F	S	S
1	2	3	4	5	6	7
8	9	10	11	12	13	14
15	16	17	18	19	20	21
22	23	24	25	26	27	28
29	30	31				

August						
M	T	W	T	F	S	S
				1	2	3	4
5	6	7	8	9	10	11
12	13	14	15	16	17	18
19	20	21	22	23	24	25
26	27	28	29	30	31	

September						
M	T	W	T	F	S	S
						1
2	3	4	5	6	7	8
9	10	11	12	13	14	15
16	17	18	19	20	21	22
23	24	25	26	27	28	29
30						

October						
M	T	W	T	F	S	S
1	2	3	4	5	6	
7	8	9	10	11	12	13
14	15	16	17	18	19	20
21	22	23	24	25	26	27
28	29	30	31			

November						
M	T	W	T	F	S	S
				1	2	3
4	5	6	7	8	9	10
11	12	13	14	15	16	17
18	19	20	21	22	23	24
25	26	27	28	29	30	

December						
M	T	W	T	F	S	S
						1
2	3	4	5	6	7	8
9	10	11	12	13	14	15
16	17	18	19	20	21	22
23	24	25	26	27	28	29
30	31					

Practice

Look at the events at the Smith Auditorium.
Complete the sentences.

Example: The party is in ___April___.

1. The play is in _____.

2. The movie is in _____.

3. The concert is in _____.

🎧 *Now listen and check your work.*

1999 Events / Smith Auditorium

January 15–20
    Steel Dragon Rock Concert

February 3–5
    Movie: Gone With the Wind
☐
March 1
    Play: Hamlet

April 12
    Party

Seasons

🎧 *Look at the pictures. Listen. Say each word.*

the spring

the summer

the fall

the winter

LISTENING WITH A PURPOSE

🎧 *Look at the chart. Listen.*

Day	Event	Time
Sunday	movie	8:00
Monday		
Tuesday		
Wednesday		
Thursday		
Friday		
Saturday		

🎧 *Now listen again. Complete the chart.*

SOCIAL LANGUAGE AND GRAMMAR 1

Conversation

🎧 *Listen and read.*

A: Hello?

B: Hello, David? This is Ben.

A: Oh, hi, Ben.

B: Is Mary Ann there?

A: No, she's not. She's at the movies.

B: OK. I'll call back later.

🎧 *Listen again and practice.*

Pair Practice

Practice the first part of the conversation with a partner. Use your own words.

A: Hello?

B: Hello, _____? This is _____.

A: Oh, hi, _____.

Now practice the rest. Use your own words.

B: Is _____ there?

A: No, _____ not. _____ at _____.

B: OK. I'll call back later.

Now practice it all.

A: Hello?

B: Hello, _____? This is _____.

A: Oh, hi, _____.

B: Is _____ there?

A: No, _____ not. _____ at _____.

B: OK. I'll call back later.

SOCIAL LANGUAGE AND GRAMMAR 2

Grammar Practice

Look at the picture. Write three more sentences.

EVENTS

Sunday — Soccer Game, 2:00 P.M.

Wednesday — Movie, 7:30 P.M.

Thursday — Concert, 8:00 P.M.

Saturday — Party, 7:30 P.M.

Example: There's a movie on Wednesday at 7:30. _____

1. _____

2. _____

3. _____

Conversation

🎧 *Listen and read.*

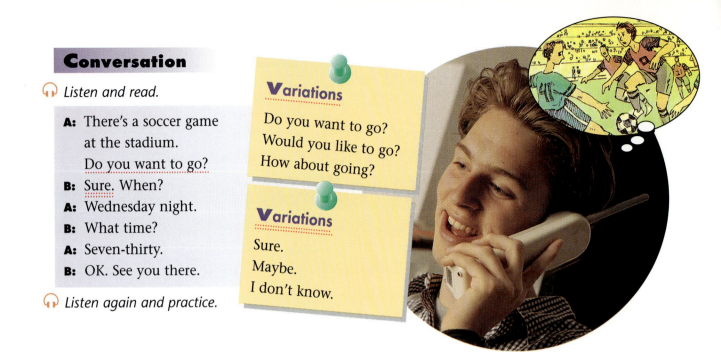

A: There's a soccer game at the stadium.
Do you want to go?
B: Sure. When?
A: Wednesday night.
B: What time?
A: Seven-thirty.
B: OK. See you there.

🎧 *Listen again and practice.*

Variations

Do you want to go?
Would you like to go?
How about going?

Variations

Sure.
Maybe.
I don't know.

Questions with When and What Time	
questions	**answers**
When is the concert?	It's on Friday. (*or* On Friday.)
What time?	It's at 8 P.M. (*or* At 8 P.M. *or* 8 P.M.)

Pair Practice

Practice with a partner. Use your own words.

A: There's a _____ at _____.

Do you want to go?

B: Sure. When?

A: _____.

B: What time?

A: _____.

B: OK. See you there.

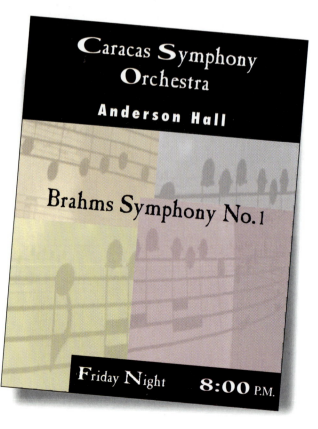

Caracas Symphony Orchestra

Anderson Hall

Brahms Symphony No.1

Friday Night   8:00 P.M.

Improvise

Tell your partner about an event.
Then invite your partner to the event.

SOCIAL LANGUAGE AND GRAMMAR 3

Conversation

🎧 *Listen and read.*

A: Hey, Caroline. What time is it?
B: It's eight-fifteen.
A: Uh-oh. I'm late. Bye.
B: Bye.

🎧 *Listen again and practice.*

Variations

Bye.
Good-bye.
Take care.
See you.

Pair Practice

Practice with a partner. Use your own words.

A: Hey, _____. What time is it?

B: It's _____.

A: Uh-oh. I'm late. Bye.

B: _____.

LISTENING WITH A PURPOSE

🎧 *Listen.*

🎧 *Now listen again. Circle the correct answer.*

1. The man is _____.   **a.** Bill   **b.** Will

2. The woman is _____.   **a.** Mary   **b.** Sally

3. The movie is _____.   **a.** *Star Wars 9*   **b.** *Star Trek 12*

4. The time is _____.   **a.** 7:15   **b.** 7:45

5. The phone number is _____.   **a.** 448-7021   **b.** 448-7012

Expansion Inter-Action — Answer the Question

Partner A: Ask Partner B five questions.
Partner B: Choose the correct answer.
Tell Partner A.

Partner B: Ask Partner A five questions.
Partner A: Choose the correct answer.
Tell Partner B.

Partner A's questions

Is the party tonight?
Is today Wednesday?
How are you?
What's your address?
Who's your teacher?

Partner B's questions

What time is it?
Are you a student?
What's your name?
When is the basketball game?
Is it 5:00?

Partner B's answers

No, today is Thursday.
1020 Main Street.
Fine, thanks.
Mr. Lee.
Yes, it's tonight at 6:00.

Partner A's answers

Three o'clock.
On Saturday.
No. I'm a teacher.
Jack Sun.
No, it's 4:30.

- Talk about the people and events.
  Example: *There's a concert on Friday at 8:00.*

- Ask and answer questions.
  Example: A: *When is the soccer game?*
  B: *It's on Friday.*

- Create a conversation for the man and the woman.
  Example: A: *There's a soccer game tonight. Do you want to go?*
  B: *What time?*

In Your Own Words

Unit 5

He's watching TV.

THE HOUSE
VOCABULARY

Furniture and Appliances

🎧 *Look at the pictures. Listen. Say each word.*

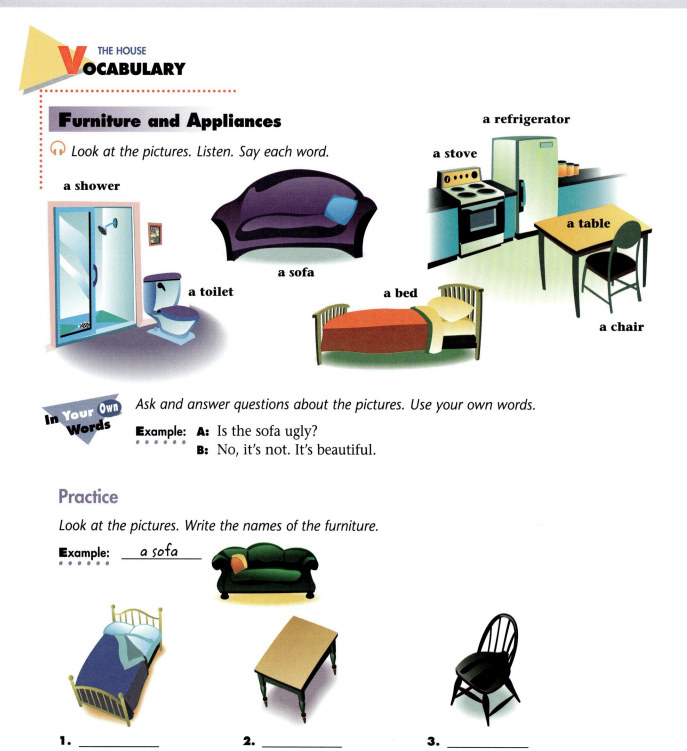

a shower

a toilet

a sofa

a bed

a stove

a refrigerator

a table

a chair

In Your Own Words *Ask and answer questions about the pictures. Use your own words.*

Example: **A:** Is the sofa ugly?

B: No, it's not. It's beautiful.

Practice

Look at the pictures. Write the names of the furniture.

Example: ___a sofa___

1. _____

2. _____

3. _____

🎧 *Now listen and check your work.*

Other Things in the House

🎧 *Look at the picture. Listen. Say each word.*

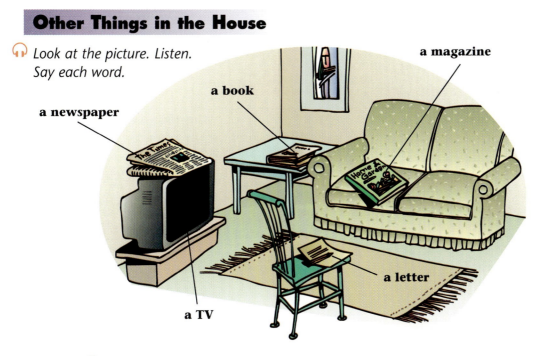

a newspaper

a book

a magazine

a TV

a letter

 With a partner, talk about the picture. Use your own words.

Example: There's a book on the table.

Practice

Look at the picture. Answer the questions.

Example: Where's the newspaper?
<u>It's on the table.</u>

1. Where's the letter?

_____

2. Where's the magazine?

_____

3. Where's the book?

_____

🎧 *Now listen and check your work.*

Rooms in the House

🎧 *Look at the pictures. Listen. Say each word or phrase.*

the kitchen

the dining room

the living room

the bedroom

 With a partner, talk about the pictures. Use your own words.

Example: There's a TV in the bedroom.

Practice

*Look back at **Rooms in the House**. Complete the conversations.*

Example: **A:** Where's Mom?

            B: She's ___in the kitchen___.

1. A: Where's the newspaper?

     B: It's _____.

2. A: Where's Dad?

     B: He's _____.

🎧 *Now listen and check your work.*

Activities in the House

🎧 *Look at the pictures. Listen. Say each word and sentence.*

read
Mrs. Kline **is reading** a book.

write
Her husband **is writing** a letter.

eat
Shelly **is eating**.

watch
Nick **is watching** TV.

study
Mike **is studying**.

work
The businessman **is working**.

sleep
Carol **is sleeping**.

shave
Brian **is shaving** in the bathroom.

Meals

🎧 *Look at the pictures. Listen. Say each word.*

breakfast   **lunch**   **dinner**

With a partner, talk about a picture. Point. Use your own words.

Example: It's 8:00. She's eating breakfast.
• • • • • •

Practice

Look at the pictures. Complete the sentences.

Example: She's eating ___breakfast___ .

1. He's eating _____.

2. She's eating _____ in the living room.

3. She's in the dining room. She's eating _____.

🎧 *Now listen and check your work.*

LISTENING WITH A PURPOSE

Receptive Model

🎧 *Look at the pictures. Listen.*

a. _____

b. _____

c. _____

🎧 *Now listen again. Number the pictures 1, 2, and 3.*

The Present Continuous		
full form		**contractions**
I *am eating.*	=	I'm eating.
He *is eating.*	=	He's eating.
She *is eating.*	=	She's eating.
We *are eating.*	=	We're eating.
You *are eating.*	=	You're eating.
They *are eating.*	=	They're eating.

TIP: eat + *-ing* = eating

write + *-ing* = writing

Grammar Practice 1

Write sentences. Use the present continuous. Write the full form.

Example: I / eat _____ I am eating. _____

1. She / write _____

2. They / read / a book _____

3. I / eat / breakfast right now _____

Grammar Practice 2

Write sentences. Use the present continuous. Use contractions.

Example: I / eat _____ I'm eating. _____

1. We / write / a book _____

2. He / study / in his bedroom _____

3. I / watch / TV _____

Conversation

🎧 *Listen and read.*

A: Hello?

B: Hi, Kevin. Are you busy?

A: Well, I'm eating lunch right now.
Can I call you back later?

B: Sure. No problem.

🎧 *Listen again and practice.*

Variations

Sure. No problem.
Fine.
OK.

Pair Practice

Practice with a partner. Use your own words.

A: Hello?

B: Hi, _____. Are you busy?

A: Well, I _____ right now.

Can I call you back later?

B: _____.

SOCIAL LANGUAGE AND GRAMMAR 2

Conversation

🎧 *Listen and read.*

A: Excuse me. Are you busy?

B: Oh, hi, Diane.
No, I'm not working right now.
I'm just reading the newspaper.
Come in.

🎧 *Listen again and practice.*

Pair Practice

Practice with a partner. Use your own words.

A: Excuse me. Are you busy?

B: Oh, hi, _____. No, I'm not working right now.

I'm just _____. Come in.

The Present Continuous: Negative	
full form	**contractions**
I am not eating.	I'm not eating.
He is not eating.	He's not eating. (*or* He isn't eating.)
We are not eating.	We're not eating. (*or* We aren't eating.)
You are not eating.	You're not eating. (*or* You aren't eating.)
They are not eating.	They're not eating. (*or* They aren't eating.)

SOCIAL LANGUAGE AND GRAMMAR 3

The Present Continuous: Yes-No Questions and Short Answers		
questions	**affirmative**	**negative**
Are you working?	Yes, I am.	No, I'm not.
Is she working?	Yes, she is.	No, she's not. (*or* No, she isn't.)
Are they working?	Yes, they are.	No, they're not. (*or* No, they aren't.)

Conversation

🎧 *Listen and read.*

A: Hello?

B: Hi, Christa? Robert. Are you eating dinner?

A: No, we're not.

B: Well, is Tony there?

A: Sure. Just a minute. Hold on. . . . Tony, it's for you.

🎧 *Listen again and practice.*

Pair Practice

Practice with a partner. Use your own words.

A: Hello?

B: Hi, _____? _____. Are you _____?

A: No, _____.

B: Well, is _____ there?

A: Sure. Just a minute. Hold on. . . . _____, it's for you.

SOCIAL LANGUAGE AND GRAMMAR 4

The Present Continuous: Wh- Questions	
questions	answers
What's he reading?	A magazine.
Where's he studying?	In the kitchen.
Why is he studying in the kitchen?	Because Sandra is in the living room.

Conversation

🎧 *Listen and read.*

A: Where's Dad?
B: He's in the kitchen.
A: What's he doing?
B: He's reading.
A: Why is he reading in the kitchen?
B: Because Adam's watching TV in the living room.

🎧 *Listen again and practice.*

Pair Practice

Practice with a partner. Use your own words.

A: Where's _____?

B: _____.

A: What's _____ doing?

B: _____.

A: Why is _____?

B: Because _____.

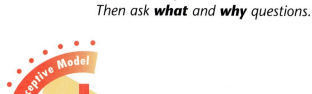

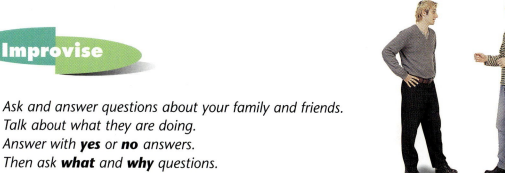

Ask and answer questions about your family and friends.
Talk about what they are doing.
Answer with **yes** or **no** answers.
Then ask **what** and **why** questions.

LISTENING WITH A PURPOSE

Read the questions about Bob. Listen. Answer the questions.

1. Where is he? _____

2. What's he doing? _____

You and your partner have a picture of the same house.
Partner A, your picture is on page 138.
Partner B, your picture is on page 139.
Ask and answer questions.

Example: **A:** What time is it in your picture?
B: One o'clock.
A: What time is it in your picture?
B: It's twelve o'clock.
A: Who's in the living room now?
B: . . .

READING AND WRITING

A Letter

Mary is a nursing student. She's studying in Chicago now. She's writing a letter to her mother and father in Jamaica.

Before you read, look at the picture. Where is Mary?

🎧 *Read the letter.*

Wednesday

Dear Mom and Dad,

How's it going? I'm fine. Chicago is great. How's Susie? Is her new school good?

Well, it's six-thirty in the morning, and here I am on the bus to the hospital. There are seven other people on the bus. Six people are sleeping, and a young man is shaving. That's right. He's shaving on the bus. I'm not joking!

I love Chicago. The buildings are big and beautiful.

My new telephone number is (773) 555-0981, and my new address is 5045 North Paulina.

Please call and write.

Love,
Mary

Now write a letter to your family or to a good friend.

Dear _____,

How's it going?

_____

_____

_____

_____

_____

_____

- Talk about the people and things.
  Example: *There's a TV in the bedroom.*

- Ask and answer five questions.
  Begin with **Is, Are, Who, What,** and **Where.**
  Example: *A: Who is in the living room?*
              B: Matt and John.

- Make false statements with the present continuous.
  Correct your partner's statements.
  Example: *A: Felix is watching TV.*
              B: No. He's not watching TV. He's shaving.

In Your Own Words

Review, SelfTest, and Extra Practice

PART 1

Review

🎧 *Read or listen to this article about the actor Ron Shore.*

Ron Shore is an actor from London, England. He's married to the beautiful singer Lucia Jones. Ron and Lucia's house is in Los Angeles, California.

Ron is on TV at 2:00 in the afternoon. He's on *Central Hospital.* On TV, Ron is Dr. Tim Blair.

Right now, Ron and Lucia are watching *Central Hospital.*

SelfTest

Check (√) **true, false,** or **I don't know.**

	True	False	I don't know.
Example: Ron is a doctor.	☐	☑	☐
1. Ron is from the United States.	☐	☐	☐
2. Lucia is from England.	☐	☐	☐
3. Lucia and Ron are married.	☐	☐	☐
4. It is afternoon now.	☐	☐	☐
5. Ron is not a singer.	☐	☐	☐
6. In the picture, Ron and Lucia are eating breakfast.	☐	☐	☐

WRITING

Create a story about Lucia Jones. In your story, answer these questions.

Who is Lucia Jones?
Where is she from?
Is she young? old? beautiful?
Is her house big or small?
Where is she now? What is she doing?

Example: Lucia Jones is a singer. She is from _____.

Extra Practice

PART 2

Review

🎧 *Listen to these telephone messages.*

SelfTest

🎧 *Now listen again. Circle the correct phone number.*

Amy:	456-9090	457-9020	457-9090
Mom:	789-0898	789-0989	799-0989
Helen Gamboa:	870-3290	870-2290	870-2390

Improvise

Work with three students.

Partner A, ask questions about names, phone
numbers, and occupations.
Partners B, C, and D answer.

Example:
A: What's your name?
B: David Banks.
A: What's your address?
B: 25 East Avenue.
A: What's your name?
C: Marlene Schneider. . . .

Now Partner B asks questions.
Partner A answers.

PART 3

Review

*Marvin and Nancy Winston are at Dan and
Janet Baker's house. Dan and Janet are in the kitchen.
Marvin and Nancy are in the living room.*

 *Listen to Marvin and Nancy.*

🎧 *Now listen again. Circle the furniture in the living room.*

a sofa	beds	a TV	chairs	a table

VOCABULARY

Complete the chart. Use the words from the box.

bank	belt	father	living room	sofa	wallet
bedroom	daughter	gym	nurse	supermarket	wife
bed	~~engineer~~	kitchen	purse	toilet	writer

Occupations	Family	Places	Personal Items	Furniture and Appliances	Rooms in the House
engineer					

Now complete this chart. Use your own words.

Occupations	Family	Places	Personal Items	Furniture and Appliances	Rooms in the House

Extra Practice

PART 4

Review

Read the calendar of events.

Calendar of Events

a.

• Movie •
The Big Chill

Cineplex
Movie Theater

Thursday and Friday
8 p.m.

b. Basketball Game
Reds vs. Tigers

Place: Gym
Friday Night—8:30

c. Concert
SISTERS AND
BROTHERS

Library
Saturday Afternoon
2 p.m.

d. Soccer Game
Place: Stadium
Time: Friday Afternoon
4:30

SelfTest

Write four sentences about the events.

Example: There's a basketball game on Friday at eight-thirty.

1. _____

2. _____

3. _____

4. _____

Work with a partner. Look at the calendar of events on page 66 again.

Partner A, choose event a or b. Invite your partner to one activity.

Partner B, choose event c or d. Invite your partner to one activity.

Example: **A:** There's a basketball game on Friday.
Do you want to go?
B: Sure. What time?
A: Eight-thirty.
B: . . .

GRAMMAR SelfTest

Present Continuous

Complete the conversations about Julia and Tom. Use contractions where possible.

1. A: _____ ?
Julia / read

   B: Yes, _____ .

2. A: _____ ?
What / read

   B: She _____ a magazine.
read

3. A: _____ the magazine?
Where / read

   B: In the kitchen.

4. A: And _____ ?
what / Tom / do

   B: _____ in the kitchen.
He / shave

5. A: _____ in the kitchen?
Why / shave

   B: I don't know.

Affirmative and Negative

Complete the sentences. Use the verbs in parentheses.
Make one verb negative. Use contractions.

Example: They_re not reading_____. They_re writing_____. (read / write)

1. He _____. He _____ TV. (sleep / watch)

2. We _____. We _____ lunch. (work / eat)

Wh- Questions

*Complete the questions. Use **Who, What, Where, When,** or **Why.***

Example: **A:** ___Where___ is the basketball game?

B: At the gym.

1. **A:** _____ are they?

   B: They're my sons.

2. **A:** _____ is the concert?

   B: Eight o'clock tonight.

3. **A:** _____ are you?

   B: I'm at work.

4. **A:** _____ is he doing?

   B: He's watching TV.

5. **A:** _____ are you eating dinner at 5:00?

   B: Because there's a soccer game at 6:00.

Practice with a partner.
Partner A, ask a question.
Partner B, answer the question.

Partner A

Partner B

Example: What's your phone number?

a. 778-1046.

b. What about you?

c. A–L–A–N.

1. How's it going?

a. John Harris.

b. Fine, thanks.

c. Seven.

2. Where's the gym?

a. On Main Street.

b. He's at the supermarket.

c. Thanks.

3. Are you Bill?

a. B–I–L–L.

b. I'm an engineer.

c. No, I'm not. I'm Jim.

4. That's a beautiful ring. Is it from Japan?

a. Tokyo.

b. No, I'm not.

c. No, it's not.

5. What time is the basketball game?

a. It's at the gym.

b. It's at 7:00 P.M.

c. No, it's tonight.

6. Is Bob there?

a. Sure. Hold on. Bob, it's for you.

b. OK. Fine. No problem.

c. Can I call you back later?

Now, Partner B, start.
Partner A, respond.

Partner B

1. What's your name?

2. Where are you from?

3. Frank, this is my brother, Ken.

4. When is the play?

5. Why is Dad reading in the living room?

6. What do you do, Pat?

Partner A

a. Sally Smith.
b. Great.
c. I'm a teacher.

a. The kitchen.
b. At the post office.
c. Mexico.

a. Are you Ken?
b. I'm not Ken.
c. Nice to meet you, Ken.

a. Sure.
b. At the theater.
c. Tomorrow at 8:00.

a. Because Mom's sleeping in the bedroom.
b. No problem.
c. He's not in the dining room.

a. 405–9981.
b. I'm a writer.
c. Nice to meet you.

EATING AND DRINKING
VOCABULARY

Drinks

🎧 *Look at the pictures. Listen. Say each word.*

☐ coffee	☐ tea	☐ soda	☐ water	☐ milk	☐ juice

In Your Own Words

With a partner, talk about a picture. Point. Use your own words.

Example: She's drinking soda.

Practice

🎧 *Look back at **Drinks**. Listen. Number the pictures 1, 2, 3, 4, 5, and 6 in the boxes (☐).*

Hunger and Thirst

🎧 *Look at the pictures. Listen. Say each word and sentence.*

hungry

He's **hungry.**

thirsty

She's **thirsty.**

In Your Own Words

Work with a partner. Ask and answer questions.

Example: **A:** Are you hungry?
B: No, I'm not.

Practice

🎧 Listen. Complete the conversations. Use **hungry** or **thirsty**.

1. **A:** Dad, I'm really _____.

   B: How about some soda?

2. **A:** Billy, it's time for dinner.

   B: I'm not _____, Mom.

Foods

🎧 Look at the pictures. Listen. Say each word or phrase.

meat

fish

rice

pizza

soup

pasta

bread

toast

ice cream

cereal

milk

a hamburger   hamburgers

an egg   eggs

a sandwich   sandwiches

Work with a partner. Ask and answer questions.

Example: **A:** What's in your refrigerator?
B: Fish, bread, and ice cream.

Practice

Look at the pictures. Complete the sentences.

Example: He's eating <u>*ice cream*</u> .

1. She's eating _____.

2. He's eating _____.

3. He's eating _____.

4. She's eating _____.

Now listen and check your work.

Wants, Needs, and Likes

Look at the pictures. Listen. Say each word and sentence.

need	She **needs** water.
have	They **have** three sandwiches.
want	They **want** ice cream.
like	They **like** ice cream.

In Your Own Words *Work with a partner. Ask and answer questions. Use your own words.*

Example: **A:** What do you need?
B: I need coffee.

Practice

🎧 *Listen and write.*

Example: You hear, "I like pasta." You write: _____ I like pasta. _____

1. _____   3. _____

2. _____   4. _____

Receptive Model

LISTENING WITH A PURPOSE

🎧 *Listen to the statements.*
🎧 *Now listen again. Check (√) the statements you hear.*

Example: ☑ Anna wants tea.

   ☐ They want tea.

1. ☐ She's eating an egg.   3. ☐ John wants a hamburger.

   ☐ She's eating eggs.   ☐ John wants hamburgers.

2. ☐ He wants water.   4. ☐ She needs coffee.

   ☐ They want water.   ☐ We need coffee.

SOCIAL LANGUAGE AND GRAMMAR 1

The Simple Present Tense	
I, you, we, they	**he, she**
I *like* pizza.	He *likes* pizza.
You *want* ice cream.	She *wants* coffee.
We *need* water.	She *needs* water.
They *want* coffee.	
TIP: I *have* pizza.	She *has* coffee.

Grammar Practice

Look at the pictures. Complete the sentences.

1. They ___need___ coffee.
    need / needs

2. They _____ toast and eggs.
    have / has

3. The mother and the father _____ toast and eggs.
    want / wants

4. The mother _____ coffee with milk.
    like / likes

5. The daughter _____ cereal.
    want / wants

6. The son _____ pizza.
    want / wants

The Simple Present Tense: Questions		
questions	**answers**	
Do we have bread?	Yes, we do.	No, we don't.
Does Jennifer want milk?	Yes, she does.	No, she doesn't.
What do you want?	A hamburger.	Nothing right now, thanks.

Conversation

🎧 *Listen and read.*

A: Hi, Dad. How about lunch?
B: Sure, thanks. I'm really hungry.
   What do we have?
A: Hamburgers.
B: Great.

🎧 *Listen again and practice.*

Variations

Great.
OK.
Sounds good.
That's fine.

Practice with a partner. Use your own words.

A: Hi, _____. How about _____?

B: Sure, thanks. I'm really _____. What do we have?

A: _____.

B: _____.

SOCIAL LANGUAGE AND GRAMMAR 2

Conversation

🎧 *Listen and read.*

A: What's for lunch?
B: Pizza. Is that OK?
A: Well, actually, I don't like pizza.
B: You're kidding. Everybody likes pizza.
A: Not me.

🎧 *Listen again and practice.*

Variations

You're kidding.
I don't believe it.
You don't?

Pair Practice

Practice with a partner. Use your own words.

A: What's for _____?

B: _____. Is that OK?

A: Well, actually, I don't like _____.

B: _____. Everybody likes _____.

A: Not me.

The Simple Present Tense: Negative	
I **don't like** fish.	We **don't have** pizza.
You **don't need** coffee.	You **don't like** pizza.
Bill **doesn't like** pasta.	They **don't want** tea.

Grammar Practice

Look at the picture. Complete the sentences.

Example: The mother ___doesn't need___ juice.
     _____
      not / need

1. The father _____ coffee.
        _____
         not / need

2. The mother _____ coffee.
        _____
         not / want

3. The children _____ their breakfast.
        _____
         not / like

Improvise

Tell your partner about foods you like and don't like.
Ask and answer questions.

SOCIAL LANGUAGE AND GRAMMAR 3

Conversation

🎧 *Listen and read.*

A: Hello?

B: Hi, Gloria. I'm at the supermarket. What do we need?

A: We're out of milk, eggs, and juice.

B: Anything else? Do we need bread?

A: No, that's all, I think. Thanks.

B: OK. See you later.

A: Bye.

🎧 *Listen again and practice.*

Variations

Anything else?
Is that all?

Pair Practice

Practice with a partner. Use your own words.

A: Hello?

B: Hi, _____. I'm at the supermarket.

    What do we need?

A: We're out of _____.

B: _____? Do we need _____?

A: No, that's all, I think. Thanks.

B: OK. See you later.

A: _____.

Receptive Model

LISTENING WITH A PURPOSE

Practice 1

Listen. Then circle the correct answers.

1. Who is talking?

    a. a brother and sister

    b. a mother and sister

2. Where are they?

    a. in the kitchen

    b. at the supermarket

Practice 2

Read these words. Listen again.

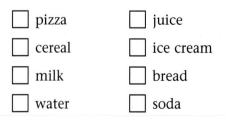

☐ pizza   ☐ juice

☐ cereal   ☐ ice cream

☐ milk   ☐ bread

☐ water   ☐ soda

Now check (√) the food they have at home.

Menu

Breakfast

Eggs	3.00
Cereal	1.50
Toast	.50
Coffee	.75
Tea	.75
Milk	1.00

Lunch

Hamburger	3.50
Pizza	8.00
Sandwich	3.50
Ice Cream	2.25
Soda	1.00
Milk	1.00
Coffee	.75

Dinner

Soup	3.00
Fish	10.00
Pasta	8.95
Ice Cream	2.25
Soda	1.00
Milk	1.00
Coffee	.75

Look at the menu. Ask a partner what he or she wants for breakfast, lunch, and dinner. Then write sentences about what your partner wants.

Example: **A:** Do you want eggs?

B: No, I don't.

She doesn't want eggs.

_____

_____

_____

_____

_____

In **Your** Own Words

- Talk about the people and things.
  Example: *The daughter wants ice cream.*
- Point and ask and answer questions with **where** and **what**.
  Example: A: *Where are they?*
  B: *They're on Blake Street.*
- Create conversations for the people.
  Example: A: *What do we need?*
  B: *Well, we need . . .*

BLAKE ST.

ENTRANCE

81

Colors

🎧 *Look at the colors. Listen. Say each word.*

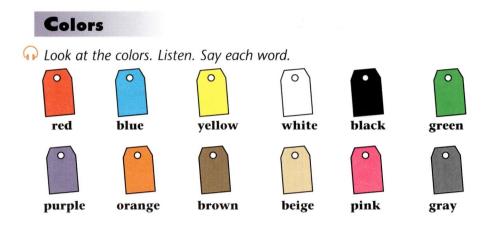

| red | blue | yellow | white | black | green |

| purple | orange | brown | beige | pink | gray |

 Tell a partner about clothes and colors you like. Use your own words.

Examples: I like purple jeans.
I like green.

Practice

Work with a partner. Look at the clothes on page 82. What colors are they?
Tell your partner.

Example: The shirt is white, and the sweater is red.

Adjectives

🎧 *Look at the pictures. Say each word.*

| dirty | clean | torn | colorful |

| comfortable | tight | loose |

 With a partner, talk about a picture. Point. Use your own words.

Example: The shirt is colorful.

Practice 1

Look at the pictures. Listen. Number the pictures 1, 2, and 3.

a. _____

b. _____

c. _____

Practice 2

Look at the pictures. Complete the sentences.

Example: Colleen's _____*shoes*_____ are small,

but her _____*hat*_____ is big.

1. Carol's _____ are new,

but her _____ is old.

2. Jason's _____ is cheap,

but his _____ is expensive.

Now listen and check your work.

Colors

🎧 *Look at the colors. Listen. Say each word.*

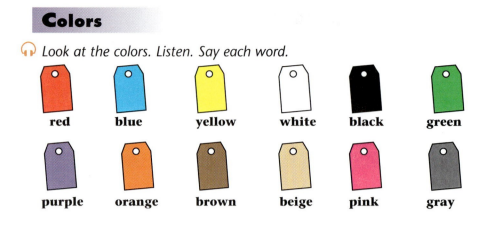

red **blue** **yellow** **white** **black** **green**

purple **orange** **brown** **beige** **pink** **gray**

 *Tell a partner about clothes and colors you like. Use your own words.*

Examples: I like purple jeans.
I like green.

Practice

Work with a partner. Look at the clothes on page 82. What colors are they?
Tell your partner.

Example: The shirt is white, and the sweater is red.

Adjectives

🎧 *Look at the pictures. Say each word.*

dirty **clean** **torn** **colorful**

comfortable **tight** **loose**

 With a partner, talk about a picture. Point. Use your own words.

Example: The shirt is colorful.

- Talk about the people and things.
  Example: *The daughter wants ice cream.*
- Point and ask and answer questions with **where** and **what**.
  Example: A: *Where are they?*
  B: *They're on Blake Street.*
- Create conversations for the people.
  Example: A: *What do we need?*
  B: *Well, we need . . .*

In Your Own Words

BLAKE ST.

ENTRANCE

81

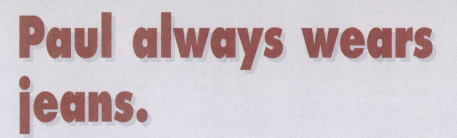

Paul always wears jeans.

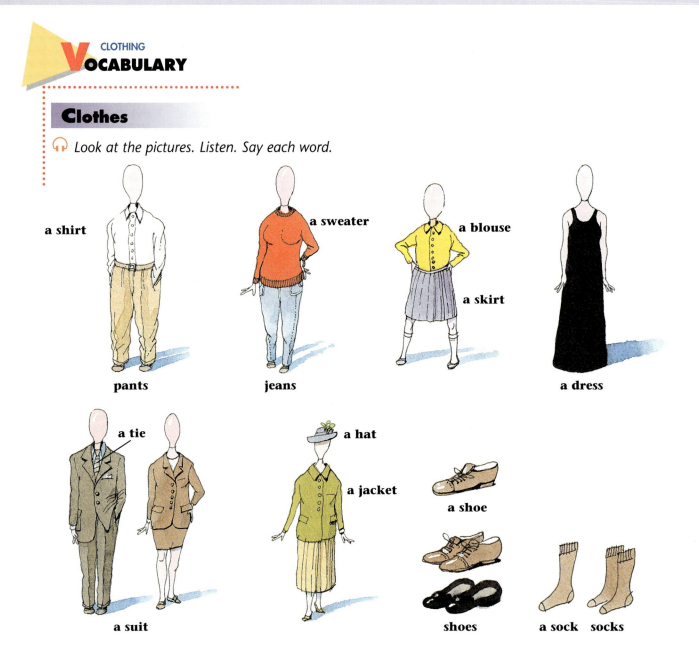

CLOTHING
VOCABULARY

Clothes

🎧 *Look at the pictures. Listen. Say each word.*

a shirt

pants

a sweater

jeans

a blouse

a skirt

a dress

a tie

a suit

a hat

a jacket

a shoe

shoes

a sock   socks

TIP: **Pants** and **jeans** are plural. (**pants**, *not* ~~pant~~)

With a partner, talk about a picture. Point. Use your own words.

Example: She's wearing a sweater.
         He's wearing pants.

Practice

Complete the conversations.
Use adjectives.

Example:

> Why do you need a new shirt?

> My old shirt is _____torn_____.

> What do you need?

> I need _____ socks.
> **1.**

> Are those pants comfortable?

> No, they're not. They're too _____.
> **2.**

FITTING ROOM

> You're not wearing your shoes!

> No. They're not _____.
> **3.**

> Do you like that skirt?

> I like it, but it's too _____.
> **4.**

Now listen and check your work.

Frequency Adverbs

Look at the diagram. Listen. Say each word.

never .... usually ... always

0% .... 50% 100%

In Your Own Words

Tell a partner about yourself. Use your own words.

Example: I always wear clean socks.

Practice

Write sentences about yourself.

Example: I ___never___ wear ___a suit___ at work.

1. I _____ wear _____ at home.

2. I _____ wear _____ at the gym.

3. I _____ wear _____ at a basketball game.

LISTENING WITH A PURPOSE

🎧 *Look at the pictures. Listen to what Molly, Cindy, and Judy are wearing.*

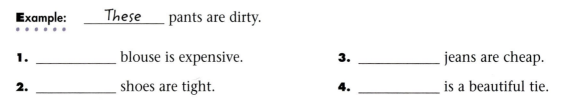

1. _____   2. _____   3. _____

🎧 *Listen again. Write each name beside the correct picture.*

SOCIAL LANGUAGE AND GRAMMAR 1

This, That, These, Those

This hat is beautiful.
I like *these* jackets too.

That shirt is dirty.
Those pants are dirty too.

Grammar Practice 1

*Complete the sentences. Use **This** or **These**.*

Example: ___These___ pants are dirty.

1. _____ blouse is expensive.

2. _____ shoes are tight.

3. _____ jeans are cheap.

4. _____ is a beautiful tie.

Grammar Practice 2

Complete the sentences. Use **That** or **Those**.

Example: _____That_____ jacket is tight.

1. _____ pants are tight.

2. _____ shirt is torn.

3. _____ is a nice dress.

4. _____ are dirty socks.

Conversation

🎧 Listen and read.

A: I like that sweater.
B: You do? Thanks.
A: It's really nice. Is it new?
B: No, it's not.

🎧 Listen again and practice.

Variations

You do?
Really?
This sweater?

Pair Practice

Practice with a partner. Use your own words.

A: I like _____ _____ .

B: _____? Thanks.

A: _____ really nice. _____ new?

B: _____ .

Improvise

Work with a partner.
Talk about clothes.

Social Language and Grammar 2

Conversation

🎧 *Listen and read.*

A: Is that Chris over there?
B: Yes, I think so.
A: Why is he wearing jeans?
B: I don't know. He never wears jeans.
A: Well, he looks <u>terrific</u>.

🎧 *Listen again and practice.*

Variations

terrific
nice
really good

Pair Practice

Practice with a partner. Use your own words.

A: Is that _____ over there?

B: Yes, I think so.

A: Why is _____ wearing _____?

B: I don't know. _____ never wears _____.

A: Well, _____ looks _____.

The Simple Present Tense and the Present Continuous	
statements	
simple present tense	**present continuous**
I usually wear a suit.	Today I'm wearing jeans.
He usually drinks coffee.	Now he's drinking tea.
We read the newspaper on Sundays.	Now we're reading a magazine.
***yes-no* questions**	
simple present tense	**present continuous**
Do you always drink coffee in the morning?	Are you drinking coffee this morning?
Does she usually wear a suit?	Is she wearing a suit today?
Do they always watch TV in the evening?	Are they watching TV now?

TIP: Don't use *want*, *need*, or *like* in the present continuous.

Grammar Practice

Complete the sentences. Use the present continuous or the simple present tense.

Example: I usually ____wear____ my gray suit. I __'m wearing__ a brown suit now
<small>wear</small>   <small>wear</small>

because my gray suit is dirty.

1. We usually _____ dinner at six-thirty.
<small>eat</small>

2. It's seven-thirty. We _____ right now.
<small>not / eat</small>

3. _____ he _____ a new suit?
<small>need</small>

4. _____ they _____ clean shoes today?
<small>wear</small>

5. My sister never _____ coffee. She _____ it.
<small>drink</small>   <small>not / like</small>

6. _____ you _____ my new jeans?
<small>like</small>

SOCIAL LANGUAGE AND GRAMMAR 3

Conversation

🎧 *Listen and read.*

A: May I help you?
B: Yes, please. How much is that black hat?
A: Forty dollars.
B: Forty dollars? That's really expensive.

🎧 *Listen again and practice.*

Pair Practice

Practice with a partner. Use your own words.

A: May I help you?

B: Yes, please. How much _____?

A: _____.

B: _____? _____.

Variations

That's really expensive.
That's too much.
You're kidding!

LISTENING WITH A PURPOSE

🎧 *Read the statements. Listen.*

		True	False	I don't know.
1.	Ms. Lang is a teacher.	☑	☐	☐
2.	Ms. Lang is wearing a pink suit.	☐	☐	☐
3.	Ms. Lang usually wears pants.	☐	☐	☐
4.	Ms. Lang is married.	☐	☐	☐

🎧 *Now listen again. Check (✓) **true, false,** or **I don't know.***

READING AND WRITING

A Description

Read the story.

Bella likes black. She usually wears black clothes. Today she's wearing a black skirt, a black sweater, black shoes, and red socks. Bella looks colorful today!

Use the story about Bella as a model. Write about a classmate.

Example: Maria likes colorful clothes. She usually wears . . .

- Point and talk about the clothes in the picture.
  Example: *I like this yellow shirt.*

- Talk about the people.
  Example: *She's tall.*

- Ask and answer questions.
  Example: A: *What's the woman wearing?*
  B: *She's wearing a sweater.*

- Create conversations for the people.
  Example: A: *I like this dress. How much is it?*
  B: *Two hundred dollars.*

Unit 8

Take aspirin.

HEALTH AND ILLNESS
VOCABULARY

Parts of the Body

🎧 *Look at the pictures. Listen. Say each word or phrase.*

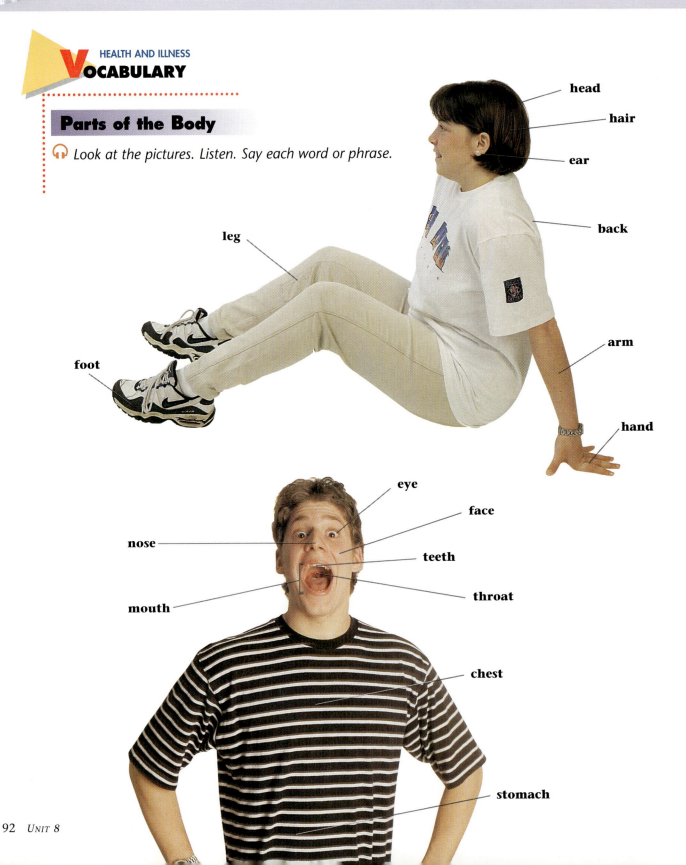

head

hair

ear

back

leg

arm

foot

hand

eye

face

nose

teeth

throat

mouth

chest

stomach

one foot   two feet   one tooth   thirty-two teeth

Practice

Look at the pictures. Complete the sentences.

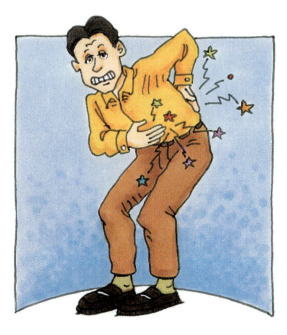

1. His ___stomach___ hurts.

2. His _____ hurts too.

3. Her _____ hurts.

4. Her _____ hurt too.

🎧 *Now listen and check your work.*

TAKE ASPIRIN. 93

Ailments

🎧 *Look at the pictures. Listen. Say each word or phrase.*

a headache

a toothache

an earache

a backache

a sore throat

a stomachache

a fever

a cold

In Your Own Words

With a partner, talk about a picture. Point. Use your own words.

Example: His head hurts. He has a headache.

Practice

Complete the sentences.

Example: Mr. Silva's back hurts. He _____*has a backache*_____.

1. Mark's throat hurts. He _____.

2. Mrs. Kelly's stomach hurts. She _____.

3. Bob's ear hurts. He _____.

4. Kathy's tooth hurts. She _____.

🎧 *Now listen and check your work.*

Feelings

🎧 *Look at the pictures. Listen. Say each phrase.*

feel sick   **feel tired**   **feel terrible**

 With a partner, talk about a picture. Point. Use your own words.

Example: She feels sick.

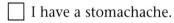

LISTENING WITH A PURPOSE

🎧 *Listen to the conversations.*

🎧 *Listen again. Check (√) the statements you hear.*

Example: ☑ I have an earache.

☐ I have a headache.

1. ☐ I have a backache.

☐ I have a stomachache.

2. ☐ My throat hurts.

☐ My back hurts.

3. ☐ I'm just tired.

☐ I'm just sick.

4. ☐ She is cold.

☐ She has a cold.

5. ☐ She still feels tired.

☐ She still feels terrible.

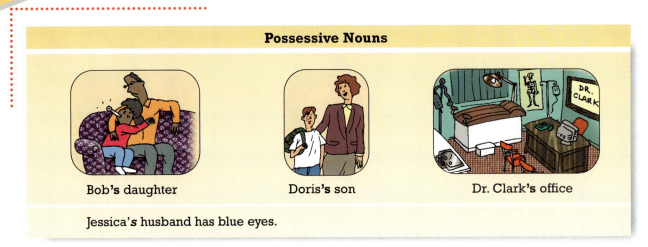

Possessive Nouns

Bob's daughter

Doris's son

Dr. Clark's office

Jessica's husband has blue eyes.

Grammar Practice

Look at the picture. Then complete the sentences.

1. This is Dr. _____ office.
        Fishers / Fisher's

2. Mrs. _____ husband has a backache.
         Carey's / Careys

3. _____ son has a sore throat.
      James's / James

4. _____ daughter has a stomachache.
       Martha / Martha's

Conversation

🎧 *Listen and read.*

A: Dr. Clark's office.
B: This is Amanda Stewart.
   I need to see the doctor.
A: OK, Mrs. Stewart. What's the problem?
B: I have a fever and a sore throat.
A: Can you come at 2:30?
B: Yes. See you then.

🎧 *Listen again and practice.*

Variations

What's the problem?
What's wrong?
What's the matter?

Pair Practice

Practice with a partner. Use your own words.

A: Dr. _____ office.

B: This is _____. I need to see the doctor.

A: OK, _____. _____?

B: I _____.

A: Can you come at _____?

B: Fine. See you then.

SOCIAL LANGUAGE AND GRAMMAR 2

Subject Pronouns and Object Pronouns

subject pronoun   object pronoun
***She*'**s looking at ***her*.**

subject pronoun   object pronoun
***He*'**s looking at ***him*.**

subject pronouns	object pronouns	subject pronouns	object pronouns
I	me	we	us
you	you	you	you
he	him	they	them
she	her		

Grammar Practice

Complete the conversations. Use object pronouns.

Example: **A:** What's Shelly doing?

B: I don't know. Why don't you ask ___her___?

Why are you looking at _____?
1.

Because I like your hat.

How about 4:30, Mrs. Summers?

Yes, that's fine. See _____ then.
2.

Where's Mike?

I don't know. I don't see _____.
3.

Do you know _____?
4.

Yes. They're my neighbors.

Conversation

🎧 *Listen and read.*

A: You don't look so good. Are you OK?

B: No. I feel terrible.

A: What's wrong?

B: I have a terrible cold.

A: That's too bad. Who's your doctor?

B: Tom Park.

A: Why don't you call him?

B: Good idea.

🎧 *Listen again and practice.*

Variations

I feel terrible.
I feel sick.
I feel awful.

Variations

That's too bad.
Oh no!
I'm sorry to hear that.

Pair Practice

Practice with a partner. Use your own words.

A: You don't look so good. Are you OK?

B: No. I _____.

A: What's wrong?

B: I have _____.

A: _____. Who's your doctor?

B: _____.

A: Why don't you call _____?

B: Good idea.

SOCIAL LANGUAGE AND GRAMMAR 3

Imperatives	
affirmative	**negative**
A: Is Naomi sick?	A: I feel awful.
B: I don't know. ***Ask*** her.	B: ***Don't work*** today.
Take aspirin. ***Drink*** juice.	

Grammar Practice

Look at the pictures. Complete the statements. Use imperatives.

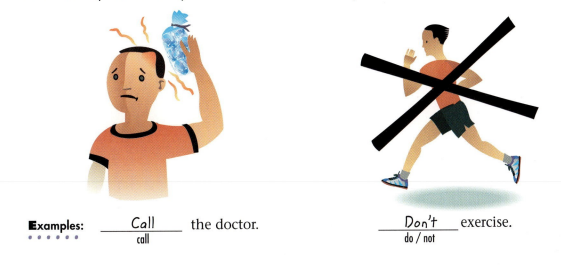

Examples: _____ the doctor.
            Call
           call

_____ exercise.
Don't
do / not

1. _____ aspirin.
take

2. _____ hot tea.
drink

3. _____ outside.
go

4. _____ a hot shower.
take

Conversation

🎧 *Listen and read.*

A: I feel awful. My back really hurts.
B: Take aspirin. That might help.
A: Aspirin?
B: Uh-huh. And don't go to work today.
A: OK. Thanks.

🎧 *Listen again and practice.*

Variations

Uh-huh.
Yes.
That's right.

Pair Practice

Practice with a partner. Use your own words.

A: I feel _____. My _____ really hurts.

B: _____. That might help.

A: _____?

B: _____. And _____.

A: OK. Thanks.

Improvise

Work with a partner. One partner is sick. Have a conversation.

LISTENING WITH A PURPOSE

🎧 *Listen to the conversation.*

🎧 *Now listen again and check (√) the correct answer.*

1. The doctor's name is _____.
- [ ] Michael Adams
- [ ] Jane Green

2. The woman's name is _____.
- [ ] Jane Green
- [ ] Michael Adams

3. The woman has _____.
- [ ] a fever and a headache
- [ ] a fever and a stomachache

4. The doctor says, _____
- [ ] "Drink a lot of juice."
- [ ] "Take aspirin."

5. The doctor says, _____
- [ ] "Eat something."
- [ ] "Don't eat anything."

6. The doctor says, _____
- [ ] "Call me later. . . . about 8:30."
- [ ] "Call me later. . . . about 9:30."

Read the chart.

Dos and Don'ts for Ailments		
ailment	do	don't
a headache	take aspirin	exercise
a stomachache	drink soda	drink milk
a backache	sleep	play soccer
a cold	drink juice	swim
a sore throat	drink hot tea	go outside

Complete the conversations. Use the chart.

1. A: My back hurts.

    B: That's too bad. Call the doctor. And _____ this afternoon.
                                                 (not)

2. A: Are you OK?

    B: No. I have a terrible stomachache.

    A: Oh, no! _____. _____.
                                                       (not)

3. A: I feel awful. I have a sore throat.

    B: Well, _____ today. And _____. That might help.
                 (not)

We Feel Terrible

You feel terrible. Tell your neighbor.
Your neighbor feels terrible too.

Example: **A:** I have a headache.
               B: Well, I have a headache and a
                     backache.
               C: Well, I have a headache, a
                     backache, and a sore throat.
               D: . . .

- Point and talk about the people.
  Example: *She feels terrible.*

- Ask and answer questions.
  Example: *A: What's the man doing?*
  B: He's calling the doctor.

- Create conversations for the people.
  Example: *A: My wife needs to see the doctor.*
  B: OK. What's the problem?
  A: . . .

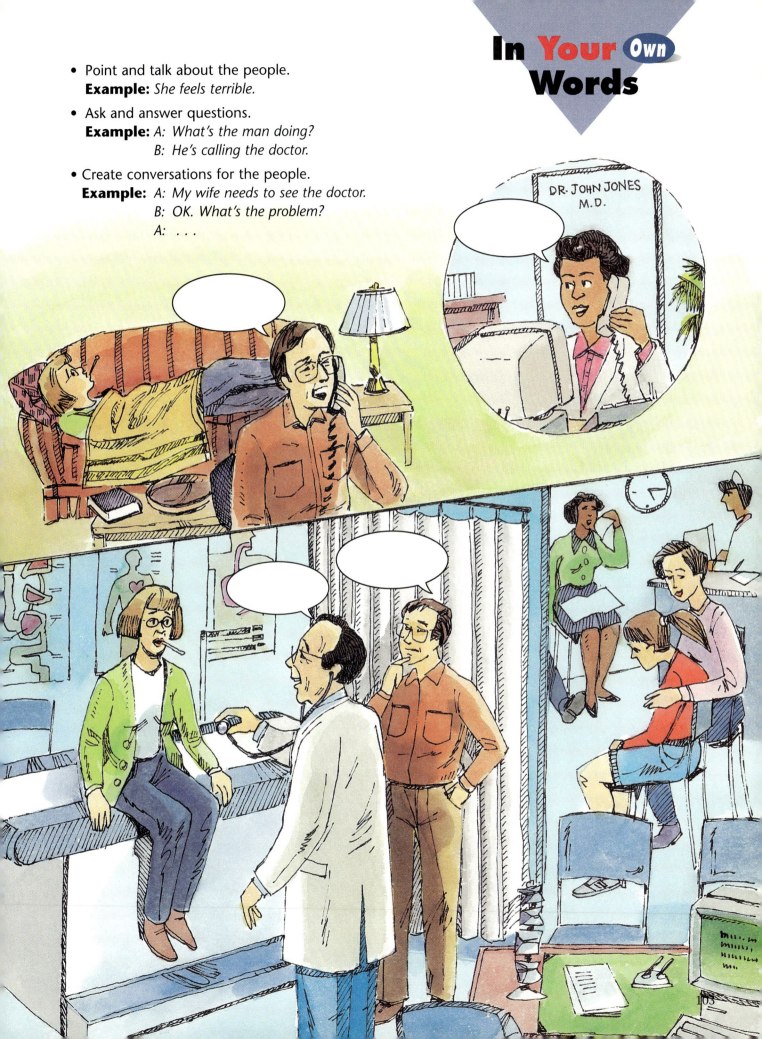

103

How was your vacation?

VOCABULARY

Past Time Expressions

🎧 *Look at the calendars. Listen. Say each word or phrase.*

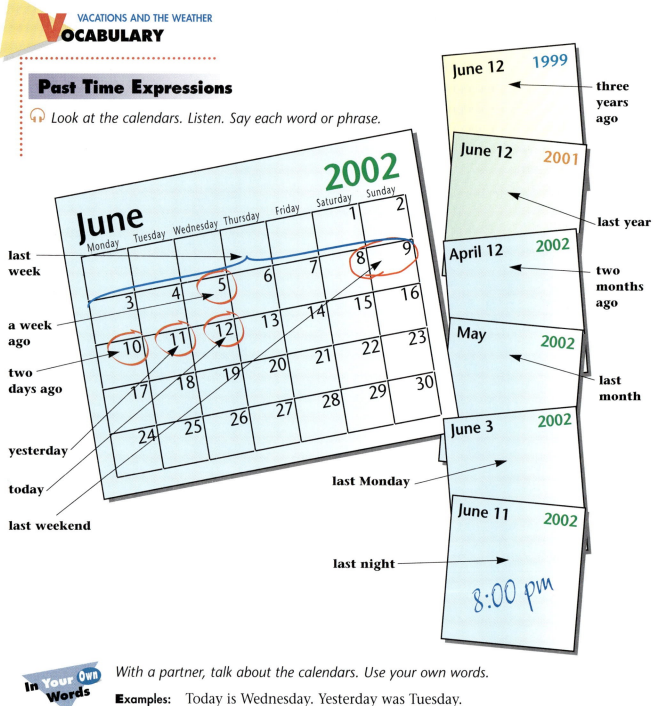

With a partner, talk about the calendars. Use your own words.

Examples: Today is Wednesday. Yesterday was Tuesday.
Last month was May.

Did you have a good vacation?

I sure did. I swam every day.

Sounds great. How was the weather?

It was beautiful.

Practice

Today is September 10. Look at Richard's calendar. Complete the sentences. Use **yesterday, ago,** *or* **last.**

Example: ___Yesterday___ Richard was at home.

1. He was in Caracas three days _____.

2. _____ week Richard was in Mexico City.

3. Richard was in Miami _____ Friday.

🎧 *Now listen and check your work.*

September

Sunday	Monday	Tuesday	Wednesday	Thursday	Friday	Saturday
					1	2
3 — Mexico	4 City —	5	6	7 Caracas	8 Miami	9 home
10	11	12	13	14	15	16
17	18	19	20	21	22	23
24	25	26	27	28	29	30

The Weather

🎧 *Look at the pictures. Listen. Say each sentence.*

It's sunny. **It's cloudy.** **It's windy.** **It's foggy.** **It's hot.**

It's warm. **It's cool.** **It's cold.** **It's raining.** **It's snowing.**

 In Your Own Words

With a partner, talk about today's weather. Use your own words.

Examples: It's cool today.

Practice

🎧 *Look at the pictures. Listen. Number the pictures 1, 2, and 3.*

a. _____   b. _____   c. _____

Places to Go on Vacation

🎧 *Look at the pictures. Listen. Say each word.*

☐ **the beach**   ☐ **the mountains**   ☐ **the country**

Practice

🎧 *Look back at **Places to Go on Vacation.** Listen.*
Number the pictures 1, 2, and 3 in the boxes (☐).

Vacation Activities

🎧 *Look at the pictures. Say each word or phrase.*

swim   **run**   **walk**

play tennis   **play golf**   **take pictures**

 In Your Own Words   *With a partner, talk about a picture. Point. Use your own words.*

Example: She's walking.

Practice

Complete the conversations. Use words from **Vacation Activities.**

Example: **A:** Does she   *run*   at the beach?
        B: Yes. Four miles every day.

1. A: Do you always _____ on vacation?

   B: No. Only when it's warm.

2. A: What do you do on vacation?

   B: Well, we _____ every day.

3. A: Do you play golf?

   B: No. But I _____.

Practice with a Partner

Ask a partner: What do you do on vacation?
Answer your partner's question.

Receptive Model

LISTENING WITH A PURPOSE

Look at the chart. Listen.

	swims	takes pictures	plays tennis	runs
husband		√		
son				
brother				
friend				

Now listen again. Put checks (√) on the chart.

SOCIAL LANGUAGE AND GRAMMAR 1

The Past Tense of Be	
singular	**plural**
I was	we were
you were	you were
he, she, it was	they were
affirmative statements	**negative statements**
I was here yesterday.	She wasn't at home this morning.
You were here too.	They weren't at work.
TIP: wasn't = was not weren't = were not	

Grammar Practice 1

*Complete the sentences. Use **was**, **were**, **wasn't**, or **weren't**.*

Alicia ___wasn't___ at work last week. She and her family _____ on vacation.
       1.   2.

They _____ at the beach. Her friends Karen and Dana _____ at work either.
      3.   4.

Karen was on vacation, and Dana _____ sick.
                                          5.

The Past Tense of Be: Questions and Answers

questions	answers
Was he at work yesterday?	Yes, he was. (*or* No, he wasn't.)
Were they in Spain last year?	No, they weren't. (*or* Yes, they were.)

Grammar Practice 2

*Complete the questions. Use **Was** or **Were**.*

Example: ___Was___ it cloudy yesterday?

1. _____ you at the beach last week?

2. _____ Barbara sick yesterday?

3. _____ they at home last week?

Conversation

🎧 *Listen and read.*

A: Where were you yesterday?
B: At the beach. Why? Were you at work?
A: Yes, I was.

🎧 *Listen again and practice.*

The Past Tense of Be: Wh- Questions

questions	answers
Where were they?	They were at work.
How was the weather?	Hot.

Pair Practice

Practice with a partner. Use your own words.

A: Where were you _____?

B: At _____. Were you _____?

A: _____.

SOCIAL LANGUAGE AND GRAMMAR 2

The Simple Past Tense of Regular Verbs

base form	simple past	
like	like**d**	We liked the movie.
rain	rain**ed**	It rained last night.
study	stud**ied**	I studied with Ruby last Sunday.

Did you ***like*** the movie?
He ***didn't study*** last night.

The Simple Past Tense of Some Irregular Verbs

base form	simple past	
come	came	Mary ***came*** to my party.
eat	ate	We ***ate*** breakfast at work yesterday.
go	went	We ***went*** to the post office two days ago.
have	had	He ***had*** a headache yesterday.
run	ran	I ***ran*** five miles yesterday.
sleep	slept	She ***slept*** in the living room last night.
swim	swam	He ***swam*** on Monday.
take	took	He ***took*** pictures at the beach.

Grammar Practice

Complete the conversations. Use the past tense form of the verb.

Example: **A:** Did you go to the beach?

B: No. I _____had_____ a headache.
_{have}

1. A: Were they at the soccer game?

B: No, they _____ at home.
_{be}

They _____ the game on TV.
_{watch}

2. A: Where were you yesterday?

You _____ at home.
_{be not}

B: I _____ to the beach.
_{go}

3. A: What _____ you _____ yesterday?
_{do}

B: I _____ a big lunch,
_{eat}

and then I _____ all afternoon.
_{sleep}

Conversation 1

🎧 *Listen and read.*

A: Did you have a nice vacation?
B: I sure did. I swam and played tennis every day.
A: Sounds terrific. Was the weather OK?
B: It was beautiful.

🎧 *Listen again and practice.*

Variations

OK
beautiful
nice
good
decent
pretty good

Pair Practice

Practice with a partner. Use your own words.

A: Did you have a nice vacation?

B: I sure did. I _____ every day.

A: Sounds terrific. Was the weather _____?

B: It was _____.

Conversation 2

🎧 *Listen and read.*

A: How was your weekend?
B: Not so great.
A: Really? Where did you go?
B: We went to the beach.
A: How was the weather?
B: Pretty bad. It was cold on Saturday, and it rained on Sunday.

🎧 *Listen again and practice.*

Variations

Pretty bad.
So-so.
Not so good.
Terrible.

Pair Practice

Practice with a partner. Use your own words.

A: How was your _____?

B: _____.

A: Really? Where did you go?

B: We went to _____.

A: How was the weather?

B: _____. It _____ on Saturday,

and it _____ on Sunday.

Improvise

Tell a partner about your weekend or your vacation.

LISTENING WITH A PURPOSE

🎧 *Listen to the conversation.*

🎧 *Listen again and circle the correct letter.*

1. Saturday's weather:
   a. It was cold and cloudy.   **b.** It snowed.   **c.** It rained.

2. Sunday's weather:
   a. It was cold and cloudy.   **b.** It was cloudy and warm.   **c.** It rained.

3. Monday's weather:
   a. It's cloudy and warm.   **b.** It's sunny and warm.   **c.** It's raining.

Who Did It?

Talk to your classmates. Ask questions. Write names.

Example: Did you watch TV last night.?

Find someone who . . .

ran yesterday _____

ate pasta last night _____

studied last night _____

went to the movies last week _____

didn't eat breakfast today _____

didn't read a newspaper today _____

didn't watch TV last night   *John* _____

WRITING

Now write about your classmates in the spaces above.

Example: *John didn't watch TV last night.*

In Your Own Words

- Point and talk about the people and places.
  Example: *She went to the beach last month.*

- Talk about the weather.
  Example: *It was cool in the mountains.*

- Point and ask and answer **wh**- questions.
  Example: A: *Where did they go last month?*
  B: *To the beach.*

- Create conversations for the people.
  Example: A: *How was your vacation?*
  B: *Great!*

LAST MONTH

TWO WEEKS AGO

115

Unit 10 I'm going to be late.

TIME AND ACTIVITIES

VOCABULARY

Time Words

🎧 *Look at the pictures. Listen. Say each word or phrase.*

early

on time

late

In Your Own Words

With a partner, talk about a picture. Point. Use your own words.

Example: It's 8:45. He's late. The class starts at 8:30.

Practice

*Complete the sentences. Use **early, on time,** or **late.***

The basketball game started at 7:30.

1. Ted came to the game at 7:45.

He was _____.

2. Sarah and Tanya came at 7:15.

They were _____.

3. Mr. and Mrs. Aponte came at 7:30.

They were _____.

🎧 *Now listen and check your work.*

Hello?

Hi, Kara. I'm sorry. I'm going to be a little late.

Where are you now?

I'm still at work.

It's OK. Take your time.

Activities

🎧 *Look at the pictures. Listen. Say each phrase.*

take a walk

go to the movies

play cards

eat out

make dinner

have a party

go to a basketball game

watch a video

stay home

In Your Own Words

With a partner, talk about a picture. Point. Use your own words.

Example: They're playing cards.

Practice

🎧 *Look at the pictures. Listen. Number the pictures 1, 2, 3, and 4.*

a. _____   b. _____   c. _____   d. _____

Future Time Expressions

🎧 *Look at the pictures. Listen. Say each word or phrase.*

today   the day after   next week
tomorrow   tomorrow   next weekend
tomorrow night   this weekend   next month

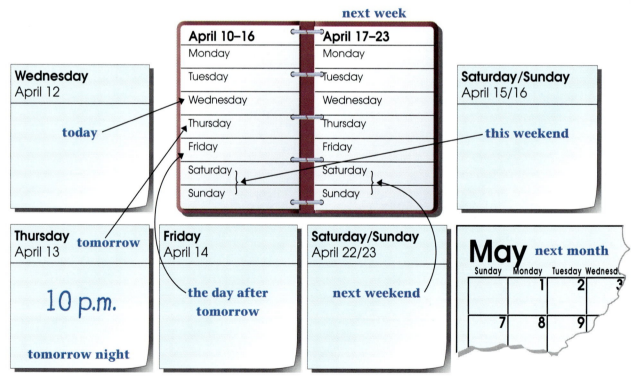

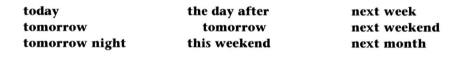

Work with a partner. Talk about the future. Use your own words.

Example: I'm going to have a party next weekend.

Practice

Look at the calendar.
Today is Monday, June 11. Match.

today

June

Monday	Tuesday	Wednesday	Thursday	Friday	Saturday	Sunday
May 1 2 3 4 5 6 7 8 9 10 11 12 13 14 15 16 17 18 19 20 21 22 23 24 25 26 27 28 29 30 31	July 1 2 3 4 5 6 7 8 9 10 11 12 13 14 15 16 17 18 19 20 21 22 23 24 25 26 27 28 29			1	2	3
4	5	6	7	8	9	10
11	12	13	14	15	16	17
18	19	20	21	22	23	24
25	26	27	28	29	30	

Tuesday, June 12

Wednesday, June 13

Saturday and Sunday, June 16 and 17

Monday–Sunday, June 18 to 24

Saturday and Sunday, June 23 and 24

July

next weekend

this weekend

the day after tomorrow

next week

next month

tomorrow

LISTENING WITH A PURPOSE

🎧 *Look at the chart. Listen.*

What?	When?
play tennis	today
have a party	
take a vacation	
stay home	

🎧 *Now listen again. Complete the chart.*

SOCIAL LANGUAGE AND GRAMMAR 1

Suggestions with Let's
Let's eat out tonight.
Let's not stay home.

Grammar Practice

*Complete the conversations. Use **Let's** or **Let's not.***

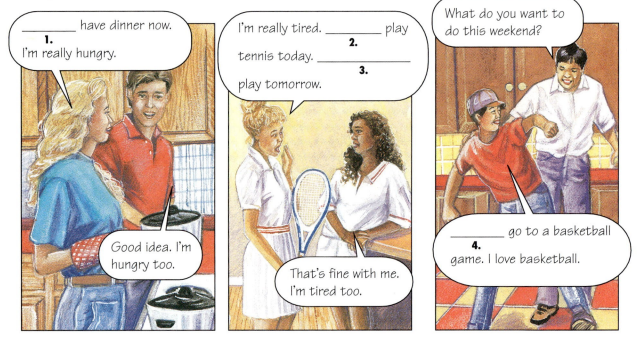

_____ have dinner now.
1.
I'm really hungry.

Good idea. I'm hungry too.

I'm really tired. _____ play
2.
tennis today. _____
3.
play tomorrow.

That's fine with me. I'm tired too.

What do you want to do this weekend?

_____ go to a basketball
4.
game. I love basketball.

Conversation

🎧 *Listen and read.*

A: Let's take a walk.

B: No, I'm too tired.

A: Well, what do you want to do?

B: Let's watch a video.

A: All right.

🎧 *Listen again and practice.*

Pair Practice

Practice with a partner. Use your own words.

A: Let's _____.

B: No, I'm too tired.

A: Well, what do you want to do?

B: Let's _____.

A: _____.

SOCIAL LANGUAGE AND GRAMMAR 2

Grammar Practice

Complete the sentences. Use a form of
be going to *and the verb.*
Use contractions.

Example: It **'s going to snow**   .

_____ snow

1. They _____

_____ a party.

have

2. She _____

_____ a dress.

buy

3. He _____

_____ TV.

watch

Conversation 1

🎧 *Listen and read.*

A: Hello?

B: Hi, Ellen. I'm sorry. I'm going to be a little late.

A: Where are you now?

B: I'm still at home.

A: It's OK. Take your time.

🎧 *Listen again and practice.*

Variations

Take your time.
Don't hurry.
No rush.

Pair Practice

Practice with a partner. Use your own words.

A: Hello?

B: Hi, _____. I'm sorry. I'm going

to be a little late.

A: Where are you now?

B: I'm still _____.

A: It's OK. _____.

Conversation 2

🎧 *Listen and read.*

A: Are you free tomorrow night?

B: I think so. What's up?

A: Danielle, Sarah, and I are going to play cards. Do you want to join us?

B: Sounds great. What time?

A: How's 7:30?

B: Great. See you then.

🎧 *Listen again and practice.*

Variations

Do you want to join us?
Would you like to join us?

Pair Practice

Practice with a partner. Use your own words.

A: Are you free _____?

B: I think so. What's up?

A: _____ are _____.

_____ join us?

B: _____. What time?

A: How's _____?

B: Great. See you then.

Conversation 3

🎧 *Listen and read.*

A: Are you going to take a vacation this year?
B: Well, yeah . . . if I have enough money.
A: Where are you going to go?
B: To Paris.
A: Really?
B: Yeah. I love Paris.

🎧 *Listen again and practice.*

Pair Practice

Practice with a partner. Use your own words.

A: Are you going to take a vacation
this _____?

B: Well, yeah . . . if I have enough money.

A: Where are you going to go?

B: To _____.

A: Really?

B: Yeah. I love _____.

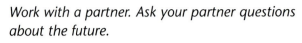

Work with a partner. Ask your partner questions about the future.

Example: **A:** What are you going to do next month?
   B: I'm going to take a vacation.
   A: Where are you going to go? . . .

Then tell the class about your partner.

Example: She's going to take a vacation.
   She's going to go to Hawaii.

LISTENING WITH A PURPOSE

Practice 1

🎧 *Listen to the conversation.*
🎧 *Listen again and check (√) the statements* **true** *or* **false**.

	True	False
1. Mary and Luke are married.	☐	☐
2. Mary and Luke are talking about tennis.	☐	☐
3. Mary and Luke are going to eat out.	☐	☐

Practice 2

🎧 *Listen again. Circle the correct answer.*

1. Mary lives in _____.

   a. San Francisco   **b.** New York   **c.** Chicago

2. Luke wants to have _____ with Mary.

   a. dinner   **b.** lunch   **c.** breakfast

3. Mary is going to be busy _____.

   a. tomorrow   **b.** this morning   **c.** tonight

4. Mary and Luke are going to meet at the Chinese restaurant _____.

   a. tomorrow night   **b.** tonight   **c.** the day after tomorrow

5. They're going to meet at _____.

   a. 6:00   **b.** 7:00   **c.** 8:00

What Are You Going to Do This Weekend?

Play as a class.

What are you going to do this weekend?

Example: **A:** I'm going to go to the movies.

B: Anne's going to go to the movies.
I'm going to eat out.

C: Anne's going to go to the movies.
Bill's going to eat out.
I'm going to . . . , *etc.*

READING AND WRITING

A Postcard

🎧 *Read the postcard.*

Tuesday, March 19

Dear Jennifer,

Vince and I are ready for a vacation! The weather here in Calgary is horrible this winter. It's snowing again today!

How's the weather in Cape Coral? We're going to be there on Saturday. It's going to be so nice to see you! On Sunday, Vince is going to play golf, and I'm going to go to the beach.

Let's play tennis every morning. And let's eat out every night. See you soon!

Love,
Alice

Now read the postcard again. Circle the correct answer.

1. Jennifer lives in _____.

   a. Calgary   **b.** San Francisco   **c.** Cape Coral

2. The weather in Calgary is _____ this winter.

   a. bad   **b.** good   **c.** OK

3. Vince and Alice are going to see Jennifer on _____.

   a. Tuesday   **b.** Saturday   **c.** Friday

4. Jennifer and Alice are going to _____ in the morning.

   a. play tennis   **b.** go to the beach   **c.** go swimming

5. They are going to _____ at night.

   a. stay home   **b.** go to the movies   **c.** eat out

Now write a postcard to a friend. Tell your friend what you are going to do.

- Talk about the people.
  Example: *The mother thinks her son is going to be a writer.*

- Ask and answer questions.
  Example: A: *What's his name going to be?*
  B: *Eric.*

- Create conversations for the people.
  Examples: A: *He's going to be a basketball player.*
  B: *No, he's not. He's going to be a . . .*

  A: *Let's name him John.*
  B: *No . . .*

In Your Own Words

Review, SelfTest, and Extra Practice

PART 1

Review

🎧 *Read or listen to this story about Stan and Martha Weiss and their young son.*

Stan and Martha Weiss had a son eighteen months ago. They named him Kevin.

Kevin likes to play, and he likes to eat. But there is one problem: Kevin doesn't sleep much. He doesn't sleep at night, and he doesn't sleep in the afternoon. Stan and Martha are always tired.

Last night Kevin went to sleep at 4 A.M. Right now it's 2 P.M. Stan is at work. He's very tired. Martha is at home. She's tired too. But Kevin is not tired. He wants to play.

What are Stan and Martha going to do?

SelfTest

Check (√) **true, false,** or **I don't know.**

	True	False	I don't know.
Example: Stan and Martha have a son.	✓	☐	☐
1. Stan and Martha's son's name is Kevin.	☐	☐	☐
2. Kevin goes to bed early every night.	☐	☐	☐
3. Kevin likes to eat.	☐	☐	☐
4. Last night, Kevin went to sleep at 10 A.M.	☐	☐	☐
5. Stan is an engineer.	☐	☐	☐
6. Stan and Martha are tired today.	☐	☐	☐

In Your Own Words

Work with a partner.
Ask and answer questions.
Talk about the picture.
Say as much as you can.

Examples: The boy is Kevin.
His hat is white . . .

Extra Practice

PART 2

Review

Listen to the conversation.

SelfTest

Listen to the conversation again. Circle the things the man is going to buy.

pasta	juice	ice cream	cereal	coffee
meat	eggs	milk	bread	fish

Vocabulary

Complete the chart. Use thewords from the box.

cereal	hand	mouth	soda
dress	juice	nose	suit
eat out	meat	pants	watch a video
go to the movies	milk	pasta	

Foods	Drinks	Clothing	Parts of the Body	Activities
cereal				

Now complete this chart with your own words.

Foods	Drinks	Clothing	Parts of the Body	Activities

PART 3

Review

 Listen to the phone conversations.

SelfTest

First look at this chart.

What?	Who?	When?
Conversation 1	Amanda	last night
Conversation 2	Jim	
Conversation 3	Martin	
Conversation 4	Mom and Dad	

Now listen to the conversations again. Complete the chart with the time words.

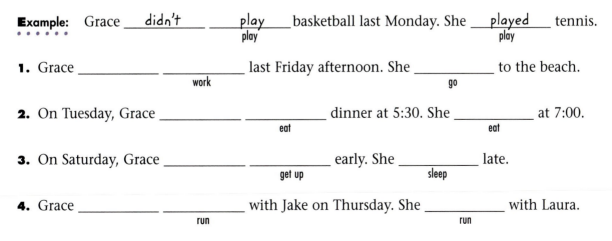
Improvise

🎧 *Listen to the conversations again.*
Work with a partner. Tell your partner about
this weekend. Then make plans to meet.

PART **4**

Review

Read Grace's calendar.

July 20–26

Monday, July 20

9:00–5:00 work
6:00 play tennis

Tuesday, July 21
9:00–5:00 work
6:00 go for a walk with Jake
7:00 eat dinner

Wednesday, July 22
9:00–5:00 work
8:00 go to a play "The
          Wild Things"

Thursday, July 23

6:00 run with Laura
9:00–5:00 work

July 20–26

Friday, July 24

9:00–12:00 work
1:00 go to the beach

Saturday, July 25

11:00 sleep late!
12:00–6:00 swim and run at
                the beach

Sunday, July 26

5:00 go home

SelfTest

Today is Monday, July 27. Look back at the calendar. Complete the sentences.
Use the simple past tense.

Example: Grace __*didn't*__ ____*play*____ basketball last Monday. She ___*played*___ tennis.
                              play   play

1. Grace _____ _____ last Friday afternoon. She _____ to the beach.
                        work   go

2. On Tuesday, Grace _____ _____ dinner at 5:30. She _____ at 7:00.
                                    eat   eat

3. On Saturday, Grace _____ _____ early. She _____ late.
                                    get up   sleep

4. Grace _____ _____ with Jake on Thursday. She _____ with Laura.
                    run   run

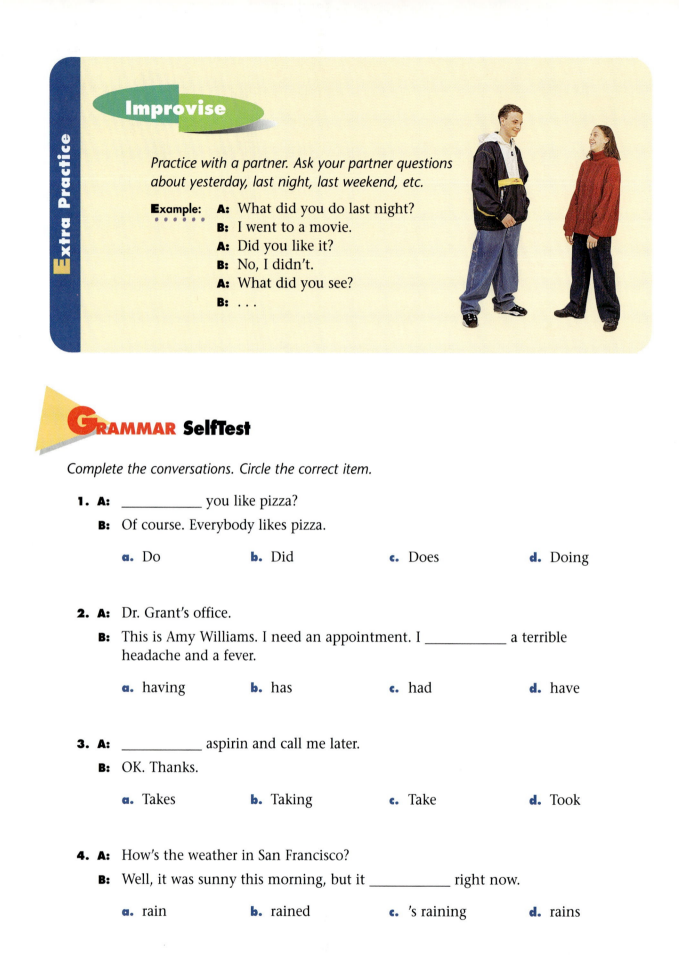

Improvise

Practice with a partner. Ask your partner questions about yesterday, last night, last weekend, etc.

Example:
A: What did you do last night?
B: I went to a movie.
A: Did you like it?
B: No, I didn't.
A: What did you see?
B: . . .

GRAMMAR SelfTest

Complete the conversations. Circle the correct item.

1. A: _____ you like pizza?
B: Of course. Everybody likes pizza.

    a. Do   **b.** Did   **c.** Does   **d.** Doing

2. A: Dr. Grant's office.
B: This is Amy Williams. I need an appointment. I _____ a terrible headache and a fever.

    a. having   **b.** has   **c.** had   **d.** have

3. A: _____ aspirin and call me later.
B: OK. Thanks.

    a. Takes   **b.** Taking   **c.** Take   **d.** Took

4. A: How's the weather in San Francisco?
B: Well, it was sunny this morning, but it _____ right now.

    a. rain   **b.** rained   **c.** 's raining   **d.** rains

5. A: Is Bill going to come to the party?

   B: I don't know. Why don't you call _____ and ask?

   a. her   **b.** them   **c.** him   **d.** us

6. A: Where _____ you last night?

   B: I was at the basketball game.

   a. was   **b.** were   **c.** wasn't   **d.** weren't

7. A: Are you free tomorrow afternoon?

   B: No. I _____ to the movies. But I'm free on Sunday.

   a. went   **b.** 'm going to go   **c.** go   **d.** goes

8. A: What's wrong? You look terrible.

   B: I feel terrible. I have a cold, and my stomach _____.

   a. hurt   **b.** hurts   **c.** hurting   **d.** is going to hurt

9. A: Why is June wearing a suit?

   B: I don't know. She never _____ suits.

   a. wear   **b.** wearing   **c.** wears   **d.** is going to wear

10. A: Who's that man?

   B: Oh, that's _____ brother.

   a. Sally   **b.** Sallys   **c.** Sally's   **d.** Sallys'

11. A: Does it rain a lot in Phoenix?

   B: No, it _____. It's usually sunny.

   a. don't   **b.** didn't   **c.** is not   **d.** doesn't

12. A: May I help you?

   B: Yes. I like _____ pants. But they're too tight.

   a. that   **b.** this   **c.** these   **d.** those

SOCIAL LANGUAGE SelfTest

Practice with a partner.
Partner A, ask a question.
Partner B, answer the question.

Partner A	**Partner B**
1. Is that Louise over there?	**a.** When?
	b. I think so.
	c. Not really.
2. Where were you last week?	**a.** On vacation.
	b. No, I wasn't.
	c. Every day.
3. How about toast and eggs for breakfast?	**a.** Sounds good.
	b. No, I didn't.
	c. Sorry.
4. Your dress is really beautiful. Is it new?	**a.** Usually.
	b. It's nice.
	c. No, it's not.
5. What's the matter?	**a.** I have a cold.
	b. Take your time.
	c. Would you like to join us?
6. Are you free tonight?	**a.** No, I don't.
	b. Sure. How about tomorrow?
	c. Yes. What's up?

Now Partner B, start.
Partner A, respond.

Partner B

1. Let's go to the movies tonight.

2. I'm going to be a little late for dinner.

3. I don't like ice cream.

4. What's for breakfast?

5. How was your weekend?

6. May I help you?

Partner A

a. No, let's not. I'm too tired.
b. I'm going to go to the movies tonight.
c. OK. Let's go tomorrow night.

a. It's OK. I'm hungry.
b. It's OK. Take your time.
c. It's OK. Do you want to join us?

a. No rush.
b. You're kidding.
c. Do you want to join us?

a. How about toast and eggs?
b. How about tomorrow?
c. How about a movie?

a. Great. I'm watching TV.
b. Great. I'm going to go for a walk.
c. Great. I went to a party.

a. Yes. How are you?
b. No, I'm not.
c. Yes. How much is that hat?

THE WORLD

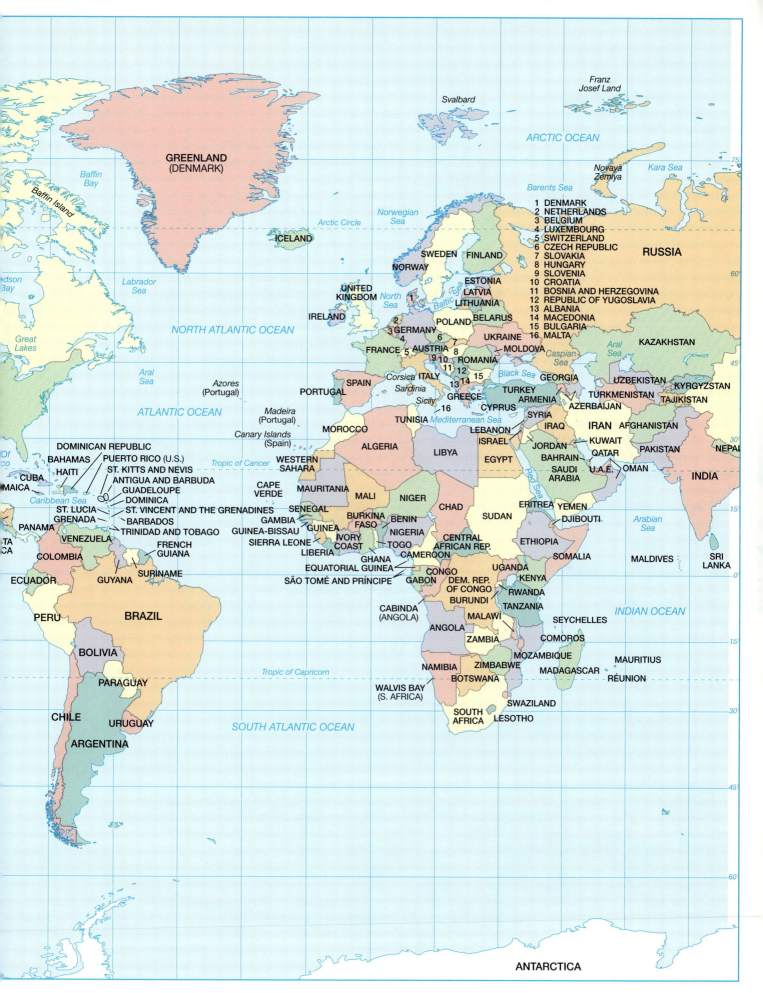

Activity Link

Appendices

Key Vocabulary

These key words and expressions were presented for active use. The definite or indefinite article is included to help students with usage.

Unit 0

Nouns

a book
a class
a letter
a partner
a picture
a question
a sentence
a word

Verbs

circle
complete
listen
look
point
read
speak
write

Directions

Listen to the conversation.
Practice the conversation with a partner.
Write your name.
Ask a question.
Answer the question.
Talk about the picture with a partner.

Social Language

Hello. I'm _____.
Hi, _____. I'm _____.
Nice to meet you _____.
Nice to meet you too.
_____, this is _____.

Unit 1

Nouns

Occupations

a businessman
a businesswoman
a doctor
a homemaker
a nurse
a singer
a student
a teacher
a writer
an actor
an artist
an athlete
an engineer

Subject Pronouns

he
I
she
you

Verbs

am
is
are

Adverb

not

Articles

a
an

Social Language

And you?
No.
What about you?
What do you do?
Yes.
Yes, I am. (No, I'm not.)

Unit 2

Nouns

Male and Female

a boy
a girl
a man
a woman

Relationships

classmates
friends
neighbors

The Family

a brother
a sister
a son
a daughter
a father
a mother
a husband
a wife

Other

name
phone number

Subject Pronouns

they
we

Adjectives

true
false
good
bad
married
single
old
young
short
tall

Possessive Adjectives

her
his
my
our
their
your

Numbers

one
two
three
four
five
six
seven
eight
nine
ten

Wh- Words

What
Who

Conjunction

and

Social Language

Fine, thanks.
Great.
Hello.
Hi.
How are you doing?
How are you?
How's it going?
OK.
Thank you.
Thanks a lot.
Thanks.
You're welcome.

Unit 3

Nouns

Places in the Community

the bank
the gym
the hospital
the library
the post office
the stadium
the supermarket
the theater

Places We Live

a building
a house
a street
an apartment

Personal Items

a belt
a briefcase
a purse
a ring
a wallet
a watch

Other

an address
an avenue
a business card

Subject Pronoun

it

Adjectives

beautiful
ugly
big
small
expensive
cheap
new

Numbers

eleven
twelve
thirteen
fourteen
fifteen
sixteen
seventeen
eighteen
nineteen
twenty
twenty-one
twenty-two
twenty-three
twenty-four
twenty-five
twenty-six
twenty-seven
twenty-eight
twenty-nine
thirty
thirty-two
forty
fifty
sixty
seventy
eighty
ninety
one hundred

Article

the

Wh- Word

Where

Prepositions

at (home, school, work)
from (country)
on (street, avenue)

Social Language

Gee!
I don't know.
Oh.
That's a beautiful
____.
That's a nice ____.
Well, . . .
What a beautiful
____!
What's the address?
Wow!

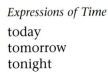

Unit 4

Nouns

Events

a basketball game
a concert
a dance
a movie
a party
a play
a soccer game

Days of the Week

Sunday
Monday
Tuesday
Wednesday
Thursday
Friday
Saturday

Time of the Day

afternoon
morning
night

Expressions of Time

today
tomorrow
tonight

Telling Time

(eight)-fifteen
(eight)-forty-five
(eight) o'clock
(eight)-thirty

Months of the Year

January
February
March
April
May
June
July
August
September
October
November
December

Seasons

the fall
the spring
the summer
the winter

Adjectives

great
late

Adverbs

later
there

Prepositions

at (the movies)
at (time)
in (month)
on (day)

Wh- Words

What time
When

Other

There are
There is

Social Language

Bye.
Do you want to go?
Good-bye.
How about going?
I don't know.
I'll call back later.
Is _____ there?
It's _____ o'clock.
Maybe.
See you.
See you there.
Sure.
Take care.
There is / are _____.
Uh-oh.
What time is it?
Would you like to go?

Unit 5

Nouns

Rooms in the House

the bathroom
the bedroom
the dining room
the kitchen
the living room

Furniture and Appliances

a bed
a chair
a refrigerator
a shower
a sofa
a stove
a table
a toilet

Other Things in the House

a book
a letter
a magazine
a newspaper
a TV

Meals

breakfast
dinner
lunch

Other

Dad
Mom

Verbs

Activities in the House

eat
read
shave
sleep
study
watch
work
write

Adjective

busy

Prepositions

in (the kitchen)
on (the table)

Wh- Word

Why

Conjunction

because

Adverbs

just
now
right now

Social Language

Excuse me.
Fine.
Hold on.
It's for you.
Just a minute.
Sure. No problem.
What's (he) doing?

Unit 6

Nouns

Drinks

coffee
juice
milk
soda
tea
water

Foods

a hamburger /
  hamburgers
a sandwich /
  sandwiches
an egg / eggs
bread
cereal
fish
ice cream
meat
pasta
pizza
rice
soup
toast

Verbs

be out of
drink
have
like
need
want

Adjectives

hungry
thirsty

Pronoun

everybody

Adverb

really

Preposition

for (breakfast)

Social Language

Anything else?
Is that all?
It's time for ____.
Not me.
See you later.
Sounds good.
That's all.
That's fine.
Well, actually . . .
What's for (lunch)?
You don't?
You're kidding.

Unit 7

Nouns

Clothes

a blouse
a dress
a hat
a jacket
a shirt
a shoe
a skirt
a sock
a suit
a sweater
a tie
jeans
pants

Verb

wear

Adjectives

clean
dirty
comfortable
colorful
loose
tight
torn
nice
terrific
really good
this
that
these
those

Colors

beige
black
blue
brown
gray
green
orange
pink
purple
red
white
yellow

Adverbs

always
never
too
usually
over there

Wh- Words

How much
Why

Social Language

I think so.
Is that (Paul)?
May I help you?
Really?
That's really
  expensive.
That's too much.
This (sweater)?
Yes, please.
You do?

Unit 8

Nouns

Parts of the Body

a back
a chest
a face
a foot / feet
a hand
a head
a leg
a mouth
a nose
a stomach
a throat
a tooth / teeth
an arm
an ear
an eye
hair

Ailments

a backache
a cold
a fever
a headache
a sore throat
a stomachache
a toothache
an earache

Other

an office
aspirin
a shower

Object Pronouns

her
him
me
them
us
you

Verbs

call
come
exercise
feel
hurt
play (soccer)
sing
take (a shower)

Adjectives

hot
(feel) awful
(feel) sick
(feel) terrible
(feel) tired

Adverb

outside

Preposition

to (work)

Social Language

Can you come at
   2:30?
Good idea.
I'm sorry to hear
   that.
I need to see the
   doctor.
Oh no!
See you then.
That might help.
That's right.
That's too bad.
What's the matter?
What's the
   problem?
What's wrong?
Why don't you (call
   the doctor)?
Uh-huh.
You don't look so
   good.

Unit 9

Nouns

Vacation Places

the beach
the country
the mountains

Other

a calendar
a vacation
the weather

Verbs

Activities

play golf
play tennis
run
swim
take pictures
walk

Adjectives

decent
not so good
not so great
pretty bad
pretty good
so-so
terrible
terrific

The Weather

(it's) cloudy
(it's) cold
(it's) cool
(it's) foggy
(it's) hot
(it's) raining
(it's) snowing
(it's) sunny
(it's) warm
(it's) windy

Adverb

every day

Past Time Expressions

a week ago
last (Monday)
last month
last night
last week
last weekend
last year
(three) years ago
(two) days ago
(two) months ago
yesterday

Prepositions

at (the beach)
in (the country)
in (the mountains)
in (Spain, Caracas)

Wh- Word

How (was the
   weather)?

Social Language

How was the
   weather?
I sure did.
Really?
Sounds great.

Unit 10

Verbs

eat out
go to a basketball
  game
go to the movies
have a party
make dinner
play cards
play tennis
stay home
take a walk
watch a video

Other

love
start

Time Words

early
late
on time

Adverbs

Time Expressions

next month
next week
next weekend
still
the day after
  tomorrow
this weekend
today
tomorrow
tomorrow night

Preposition

to (a basketball
  game)

Social Language

All right.
Are you free?
Do you want to join
  us?
Don't hurry.
. . . if I have
  enough money.
Let's (not) _____.
No rush.
Take your time.
What do you want
  to do?
What's up?
Would you like to
  join us?
Yeah.

Verbs with Irregular Past Forms

Base Form	Simple Past
buy	bought
come	came
eat	ate
go	went
have	had
run	ran
sleep	slept
swim	swam
take	took